Law In Your Life

A PUBLICATION OF

STREET LAW INC.

Law In Your Life

A PUBLICATION OF
STREET LAW INC.

Mary C. Larkin

CONTRIBUTING AUTHORS

Elizabeth Chorak

Wanda Routier

JOIN US ON THE INTERNET

WWW: http://www.thomson.com

EMAIL: findit@kiosk.thomson.com   A service of I(T)P®

West Educational Publishing

an International Thomson Publishing company I(T)P®

Cincinnati • Albany, NY • Belmont, CA • Bonn • Boston • Detroit • Johannesburg • London • Los Angeles
Madrid • Melbourne • Mexico City • New York • Paris • Singapore • Tokyo • Toronto • Washington

Production Credits

Team Leader: Robert Cassel
Consultant: Carole Grumney
Production Manager: John Orr
Editor: Lynn Bruton
Production Editor: Regan Metzler Stilo
Photo Research: Regan Metzler Stilo
Permissions: Elaine Arthur
Illustrators: Vickie Grandchamp/
 José Delgado
Copyediting: Bridget Neumayr/
 Suzie Franklin DeFazio
Design: Vickie Grandchamp/
 Matt Thiessen
Composition: Parkwood Composition
 Service, Inc.
Glossary/Index: Margaret Jarpey
Cover Design: Matt Thiessen
Proofreader: Suzie Franklin DeFazio
Prepress Services: Clarinda Company

Photo Acknowledgments

PhotoDisc, Inc.
2, 5, 9, 23, 26, 27, 33, 35, 43, 46, 64, 66, 67,
68, 97, 107, 112a, 112b, 112c, 112d, 113, 115,
120, 131, 138, 139, 155, 205, 215, 217, 221,
231, 234, 247
Corbis
36 Lynn Goldsmith/© Corbis;
50 Lynn Goldsmith/© Corbis;
57 Tim Page/Corbis;
62 W. Wayne Lockwood, M.D./Corbis;
63 Micheal S. Yamashita/Corbis;
87 Jeffry W. Myers/Corbis;
157 Richard T. Nowitz/Corbis;
160 Bob Rowan; Progressive Image/Corbis;
170 Charles E. Rotkin/© Corbis;
201 Todd Gipstein/Corbis.
Stock ◆ Boston, Inc.
79 © Billy E. Barnes.
Don Milici
117 © Don Milici, all rights reserved;
168 © Don Milici, all rights reserved.
PhotoEdit
146 © Tony Freeman.

Table of Contents

Preface

Law in Your Life addresses the needs of many youth who would benefit from practical law lessons like those offered in the textbook *Street Law: A Course in Practical Law,* but on a lower reading level. *Law in Your Life* is an outgrowth of several distinct but related practical law curricula and programs developed by Street Law, Inc. Street Law's Juvenile Court Alternative Program materials and Detention Program materials offer lessons to a specific population of students. Street Law's special education program materials are used by teachers of students with disabilities, including students who are deaf or hard of hearing. The common thread in these programs is the development of interesting, easy-to-read, practical law material that can be used by older students. Building on the success of these programs, *Law in Your Life* is for older students with high interest and cognitive needs, but lower reading skills. It is designed to provide them with practical information and competency-building activities.

Law in Your Life provides the practical information and competency-building activities that can help students analyze, evaluate, and understand legal situations in their communities. The interactive approach uses cooperative learning strategies, including small-group exercises, simulations, continuums, role-plays, and visual and auditory analysis. This approach helps develop the social skills necessary to interact with other people. Some of the social skill objectives in *Law in Your Life* are as follows:

- participate in activities with others
- accept responsibility for own actions/behavior
- empathize with others
- accept values and cultural diversity as natural.

For optimal results, *Law in Your Life* requires the participation of community resource people, such as lawyers, police officers, and school principals. This approach allows students to be active participants in their own educations. In this way, we hope to promote in students the capability and willingness to take an active role in legal and political systems.

Law in Your Life is appropriate for use in a wide variety of settings. This interesting, easy-to-read material can be used in middle/junior high or high schools, special education classrooms, and alternative education and juvenile justice settings.

Advice to Readers: The law varies from state to state and is constantly changing. Someone confronted with a legal problem should not use this text as a substitute for legal advice from an attorney.

Street Law, Inc.

Street Law, Inc., a nonprofit organization, educates people about law, democracy, and human rights in the U.S. and around the world.

Street Law, Inc., grew out of a program launched in 1971 at Georgetown University Law Center in which law students taught practical law courses in the District of Columbia's high schools. From this point, the organization expanded its programs to include alternative education settings, juvenile and adult correctional institutions, and community-based settings. Street Law's initial overseas activity—the replication of the Street Law Program in South Africa—was followed by the development of human rights and democracy education programs in virtually every country.

Street Law, Inc., promotes increased opportunities for citizens to learn about the legal system and use this knowledge to become more active participants in our democracy. Street Law, Inc., develops curricula, trains teachers, and implements programs in law-related education, democracy, and human rights. It also provides technical assistance and curriculum materials to law schools, school systems, departments of corrections, juvenile justice agencies, bar associations, legal services, community organizations, state and local government, and other groups and individuals interested in establishing law-related education programs.

In addition to *Law in Your Life,* Street Law, Inc.'s, publications include:

Street Law, A Course in Practical Law (5th ed.—1994)
Teens, Crime, and the Community (1998)
Street Law in Detention Settings (1997)
Street Law in Juvenile Court Alternative Programs (1997)
Democracy for All (1994)
We Can Work It Out: Problem Solving through Mediation (1993)
Human Rights for All (1996)
Practical Law for Jail and Prison Personnel (1987)
Great Trials in American History: Civil War to the Present (1985)
Current Legal Issues Filmstrip Series (1985)
Family Law: Competencies in Law and Citizenship (1984)
Street Law: Mock Trial Manual (1984)
Current Legal Issues Filmstrip Series (1984)

Street Law Filmstrip Series (1983)
Consumer Law: Competencies in Law and Citizenship (1982)
Law and the Consumer

For further information or assistance, please contact:
Street Law, Inc.
918 16th Street, NW
Suite 602
Washington, DC 20006
Tel: 202-293-0088
Fax: 202-293-0089
E-mail: clearinghouse@streetlaw.org
Web site: streetlaw.org

Acknowledgments

The development of *Law in Your Life* was funded in part under grants from the Office of Juvenile Justice and Delinquency Prevention, Office of Justice Programs, U.S. Department of Justice. Points of view or opinions in this document are those of the authors and do not necessarily represent the official position or policies of the U.S. Department of Justice.

The authors gratefully acknowledge the many law students, law professionals, juvenile justice professionals, secondary school teachers, and special education teachers who have assisted in the development of our curriculum materials. Over the years, many people have provided valuable field testing, research, editorial assistance, encouragement, and support to the development of *Law in Your Life* or the curriculums that led to its development. We can only name a few in the space below but we appreciate the efforts of all who have worked with us.

One of the contributing authors, Wanda Routier, is no longer part of Street Law's staff. Ms. Routier was the program director for Street Law's special education initiative. We want to acknowledge that parts of some lessons are based on her earlier writings.

While working on *Law in Your Life*, we had the assistance of several people. Elly Greene's contribution in editing both the student and teacher text was instrumental in their completion. Allison Serino also reviewed and reworked some lessons. Early in the writing of the text, Ed McMahon, a former staff member, provided us with a thorough edit of the student edition.

These classroom teachers evaluated early editions of the lessons and provided valuable input: Clare Barnett, Danbury High School, (CT); Gina Blomberg, Cherry Creek High School, (CO); Janice M. Brinkmiller, Western Hills High School, (OH); Richard Brown, Millard South High School, (NE); Joseph P. Dillon, Jr., Arlington High School, (MA); Vera Dumas, Garfield High School, (CA); Jim Gibson, Kellogg High School, (MI); Mitchell Jones, New Trier High School, (IL); Janet McGill, Edison High School, (OK); John Rhiner, Provo High School, (UT); Bonnie Sachs, Franklin D. Roosevelt High School, (NY); Janice Way, Plymouth/Salem High School, (MI).

Street Law's staff provided important assistance during the lengthy process of developing the text. Lee Arbetman played a substantial role. He supplied useful ideas and skillful technical assistance, and helped strengthen the book overall. Ed O'Brien, Street Law's co-director, edited a draft of the student manuscript and encouraged us. Judy Zimmer's support to the special education initiative and strong interest in conflict resolution made us ever mindful of the need to emphasize this area. Thanks also go to co-director Jason Newman and to Rebecca Bond who work on the finances that keep us afloat. Administrative support from the current and former staff members made this text possible. Special thanks go to Marikka Green, Beverly Powell St. James, Hellene Burnette, Loretta Humber Green, Pamela Dennis, Ana Nwaosuagwa, Nadine Blakney, and Charles Graham for their typing and photocopying support. Thanks, Deborah Foster and Karla Williams, for your administrative assistance.

One special group of individuals is committed to help Street Law, Inc., grow and prosper. They are our board of directors: Mark Gelber, President, Stuart Bindeman, Charles Kolb, Colin Greer, Janet Studley, Judge Norma Holloway Johnson, Edward O'Brien, Jason Newman, and Dean Judith Areen.

Mary C. Larkin
Elizabeth "Bebs" Chorak
Washington, D.C.
January, 1998

LESSON 1

World of Rules

After this lesson you will be able to:

➤ explain the need for rules.
➤ develop a list of guidelines for good rules.
➤ discuss laws in your life.

WORDS TO KNOW

guideline – something that instructs, controls, or directs *(noun)*

conflict – to act against *(verb)*

enforceable – able to make people obey *(adjective)*

penalty – a punishment required by law *(noun)*

code – a written collection of laws *(noun)*

privileges – special rights, favors, or advantages that are given to some person or group *(noun)*

RULES

Everyone knows you need rules in a game. Rules make games fun and fair. When someone does not play a game by the rules, it ruins the game for everyone.

What are some rules in the game of football?

A rule is a **guideline** for behavior. It is meant to manage the way a person acts or does something. For example, there are rules in the game of baseball. These rules tell baseball players how to play the game of baseball. They tell the players what they can and cannot do. Rules may be written or unwritten. They may also be started by habit or custom. For example, it is a rule in my house that we must eat dinner, at the table, together. We cannot watch television while eating. This is a family custom or habit.

Good rules are helpful, and bad rules are sometimes confusing. For example, "Do not run in the swimming pool area" is a good rule because it protects people from getting hurt. Name some good rules that you've been asked to follow. "Be friends with everyone in class" is not a good rule because it is not reasonable to order friendships. How will a teacher know if students are actually friends? Also, should there be a punishment for people who are not friends? Name some bad rules that you've been asked to follow. What makes these rules good or bad? Discuss the differences between a good rule and a bad rule.

Look at the chart below.

Guidelines for Good Rules

A. Rules should be clear and easy to understand.

B. People should be able to do what the rules say.

C. Rules should not **conflict** with other rules.

D. Rules should be **enforceable**.

E. There should be a **penalty** for breaking rules.

F. Rules should be explained to people or written in a place where everyone can see them.

Do more guidelines for rules need to be added to this list? Make a list of guidelines to add.

YOUR TURN 1-1

RULES FOR RULES

Use the **Guidelines for Good Rules Chart**. Read the following rules and decide if they are good or bad rules. Tell which guideline was broken.

1. No thinking about fighting.
2. No can from here.
3. Dancing on the ceiling only after 5:00.
4. Do not talk, but please talk quietly in the library.
5. Chew gum with your top teeth only.
6. Go to sleep at naptime.
7. Be in homeroom or first hour on time.

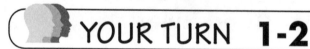

YOUR TURN 1-2

WRITING GOOD RULES

Review each rule which is poorly written in the activity above. Rewrite the rule to make it a good rule.

RULES IN THE COMMUNITY

Many places in your community have rules. In shopping malls, for example, people are not allowed to run or to play loud radio music. What is the purpose of these rules? Can you think of other places where there are rules? What are some of the rules? Why do you think these rules were made?

Name some rules that help shoppers in a shopping mall.

LAWS IN THE COMMUNITY

Laws are rules which are set and enforced by a government. They protect people and help people get along with each other. Laws are written by the government for the entire community. They are put in a **code** or law book.

Every town or city has laws. Imagine what a community would be like without laws. What might happen in a community where there are no laws?

THE DIFFERENCE BETWEEN A RULE AND A LAW

Think of a definition of a rule. Think of a definition of a law. What is the difference between a rule and a law?

Rules	Laws
A rule is a guideline for conduct or action. Rules may be written or unwritten. They may be started by habit, custom, or written guideline.	A law is written by the government.
A rule is enforced by the people who make the rule.	A law is enforced by the police, sheriff, state patrol, FBI, etc. These groups are called law enforcement.
If you break a rule, you can lose **privileges**.	If you break the law, you can be punished by the government, lose privileges or money, and go to jail.

 YOUR TURN 1-3

WE NEED GOOD RULES

Think about what you have learned about rules. Explain why rules are necessary.

1. What happens if rules are unclear?
2. What is a law? What is a rule?
3. Why are laws necessary?
4. What do you lose when you break a rule?
5. What do you lose when you break a law?

LESSON 2

Laws in the Community

After this lesson you will be able to:

➤ explain the purpose of a law.
➤ identify what a community had in mind when passing a law.
➤ discuss different explanations of the same law.

7

WORDS TO KNOW

city council – the group of people who govern a city *(noun)*

ordinances – local laws or regulations *(noun)*

unpolluted – not spoiled by trash; clean *(adjective)*

exception – anyone or anything to whom a general rule does not apply *(noun)*

CITY OR TOWN GOVERNMENT

Each city or town has a group of people who make the laws and run the city. Sometimes this group is called the **city council**. The laws made are called **ordinances**. An example of an ordinance is the dog leash law which says that dogs must be kept in a fenced area or on a leash at all times. What are some other ordinances in your city? Why are they important?

Your city is called your local government. We rely on our local government both to survive and to help us live comfortably. The local government protects us from fire and crime. It also provides us with clean water, trash collection, health services, and education.

Name two officials in your local government.

Some local governments are run by a mayor and city council. Others are governed by a county executive and a county council. The city council is elected by citizens of the city or town. The mayor may be selected by the council or elected by the citizens.

 ## YOUR TURN 2-1

Your Local Government

Read and answer the questions below. As a resource, go to the library or use the blue pages of your local telephone directory to call your government officials.

1. What is the name of the local area in which you live? Examples are a town, city, county, parish, borough, or special district.
2. What is the name of the group of people who pass your local ordinances?
3. Is your mayor or county executive elected?
4. List five local offices that are run by elected officials. Give the name of the elected official who runs each office.

Name some laws that would make parks safe for children.

YOUR TURN 2-2

NO VEHICLES IN THE PARK

Read this story about a law that a city council passed. Answer the questions at the end of the story.

Smithville has a pretty, quiet park right in the center of the city. The city council wants to make sure that the park stays safe and **unpolluted**. They do not want the park disturbed by city noise. In the park you can find grass, trees, flowers, playgrounds, and picnic areas. There is one road through the park. To make sure the park stays safe and unpolluted, the city council passes a law.

At all park entrances the following sign is posted: **No Vehicles in the Park**.

1. What does this law say?

2. Why did the city council pass the law?

3. What does the city council want to happen?

4. Will everyone understand the sign? Give your reason.

 YOUR TURN **2-3**

WILL YOU ALLOW THESE EXCEPTIONS?

Use the facts from the story you just read. Pretend you are on the city council. There are some citizens who are unhappy with the law that says "No Vehicles in the Park." Some do not understand it. Answer the following questions about each **exception**.

a. Will you allow the vehicle in the park? Give your reason.
b. What other solutions do you suggest?
c. How would you enforce your decision?
d. If you enforce the law, what is your penalty?

1. John Smith lives on one side of the town and works on the other side. He will save ten minutes if he drives through the park. John wants to drive through the park.

2. There are many trash barrels in the park. People put litter in them to help keep the park clean. The sanitation department wants to drive a garbage truck into the park to collect the trash.

3. An ambulance with a seriously injured car accident victim needs to get to the hospital fast. The shortest route is through the park. The victim may die if the ambulance doesn't go through the park.

4. Two police cars are chasing a suspected bank robber. If one police car cuts through the park, the police can trap the suspect's car between the patrol cars. The police want to drive through the park.

5. Some of the children who visit the park want to ride their bicycles there.

6. Mr. Thomas wants to take his baby to the park in a baby stroller.

7. The government donates a military tank to be placed in the park as a monument to the town's veterans who died in a war.

Your Turn   **2-3** (continued)

8. Sarah likes to go to the park with her friends. Sarah uses a
   wheelchair that has a motor. She wants to keep visiting the park.

 YOUR TURN   **2-4**

WRITING A LAW

The law "No Vehicles in the Park" is unclear. On a separate piece
of paper, write a better law which means the same thing.

LESSON 3

Civil Law

After this lesson, you will be able to:

➤ define a civil law problem.

➤ identify the difference between criminal and civil law.

➤ examine a civil case and present arguments for both sides.

WORDS TO KNOW

irresponsible – behaving in a way that can harm others; not dependable *(adjective)*

violate – to break or fail to keep a rule, law, or promise *(verb)*

private – applying to individual matters, not public ones *(adjective)*

plaintiff – the accusing person or party *(noun)*

defendant – the accused person or party *(noun)*

property – something that is owned *(noun)*

grafts – pieces of skin, bone, or other living tissue that are taken from one body and set into another so as to grow and become permanent parts of the new location *(noun)*

CIVIL RESPONSIBILITY

What do you think of when you see or hear the word *responsibility*? Responsibility is the duty to do something or not to do something. For example, Ellen ironed her blouse and turned off the iron afterwards. Ellen has a responsibility to remember to turn the iron off as protection from fire. Give some examples of something you do or don't do to protect someone or keep them from getting hurt. What happens if you don't do it?

Responsible behavior keeps our families and communities safe. A responsible person acts in the way the community or the family expects. If you do not stop to think before you act or if you forget to do something, your behavior might be **irresponsible** toward other people. You might **violate** the rights of others. You could even be breaking the law.

If a person is harmed by someone, should the person who is responsible for the injury pay the cost of medical care? If a person's property is damaged by someone, should the person who is responsible pay to repair the damage? If the responsible person does not want to pay or take responsibility for his or her actions, the person could go to civil court.

CIVIL AND CRIMINAL LAWS

Laws fall into two groups: civil and criminal. A civil law applies to two people or two groups of people. Usually one person goes to court because he or she feels wronged or injured by the other person.

A civil case is a legal action brought by one person or business against another or business. Civil cases involve settling **private** conflicts or disputes. For example, Mika Goldberg was injured in an automobile accident when the brakes on the car he was driving failed. Mika had just had his brakes repaired at Speedy Brake Repair. Mika gets a lawyer and sues Speedy Brake Repair in court. He wants the repair shop to pay for his medical bills and for the repair of his car. When Mika goes to court, the case is *Mika Goldberg versus Speedy Brake Repair.*

THE DIFFERENCES BETWEEN CIVIL AND CRIMINAL COURT

Civil Court	Criminal Court
Purpose: • To settle problems between two or more persons • To pay a victim for injury to person or damage to property	Purpose: • To protect people and society • To punish criminals • To stop illegal activity
People involved: • Plaintiff (person who sues) • Defendant (person accused of irresponsible or wrongful act)	People involved: • Prosecutor (the government goes to court) • Defendant (person accused of crime)
Punishment: • Repair or replace damaged property • Pay money to the victim • Participate in community service • Court orders a person not to behave or act in the same way again or more punishment will follow	Punishment: • Prison • Pay money (called a fine) • Probation • Suspended sentence

Some civil law cases involve family issues. Divorce, child support, and child custody are all different kinds of civil cases.

A criminal law applies to someone who breaks the law or commits a crime. A criminal case is a legal action brought by the government against a person charged with committing a crime. For example, if Ming Brown robs a store, she commits a crime. When caught, Ming will be taken by the government to criminal court. If Ming lives in St. Louis, the case will be the *City of St. Louis versus Ming Brown*.

 YOUR TURN **3-1**

THE TIGERS

Read this story. On a separate piece of paper, list the civil wrongs. Then list the criminal wrongs.

Matt and Herb argue over who should have won a professional basketball game. Matt insults Herb's favorite team, the Tigers. Matt calls the Tiger players lazy, worthless, and lucky. He says that the referee cheated. Herb gets angry. His brother is a professional basketball player on the Tigers team. Besides, Herb has been a Tiger fan for years.

Herb punches Matt in the mouth. Matt suffers two broken teeth and a split lip that requires ten stitches. Matt's dental and hospital bills total $2,000 and he misses five days of work while dental work is done. Herb needs four stitches in his hand. He also has a black eye that requires no medical attention.

CIVIL COURT

In a civil case the two people who go to court are called the **plaintiff** and the **defendant**. The plaintiff brings the case to court. He or she sues someone. The defendant is accused of doing wrong.

In some civil courts there are no lawyers, just a judge. Small Claims Court is an example of this type of civil court. Most states allow people to go to court without a lawyer if the amount of money involved is under a certain dollar amount. Usually this amount is under $500. In other civil courts both sides have lawyers to present their cases.

FILING A CIVIL LAWSUIT

If you sue someone in civil court, you must prove that the other person is responsible for doing something wrong to you. You must prove one of the following:

- That the person you sue broke an agreement which resulted in a loss of money to you.
- That the person you sue damaged your **property** on purpose, and as a result you lost money.
- That the person you sue acted carelessly or failed to act when she or he should have done so, and that this damaged you.

 YOUR TURN **3-2**

HOT COFFEE, ANYONE?

Read this actual case. Decide who was responsible for Ms. Liebeck's accident. Answer the questions that follow.

Your Turn   **3-2** (continued)

 THE CASE OF *LIEBECK* VERSUS *McDONALD'S*

Ms. Stella Liebeck orders a cup of hot coffee from the drive-in window at McDonald's. She places it between her knees. Her nephew, the driver, starts to leave McDonald's while Ms. Liebeck is putting sugar and cream in the coffee. Ms. Liebeck spills the coffee in her lap and badly burns herself.

Ms. Liebeck is 79 years old and recovery is particularly difficult. As a result of the burns, she spends eight days in the hospital and must undergo skin **grafts**. She is permanently scarred.

McDonald's coffee is very popular. It is brewed at a higher temperature than most other restaurants brew their coffee. McDonald's believes that a higher brewing temperature leads to better flavor and that its customers like hot coffee. However, McDonald's had received 700 complaints about their hot coffee from 1982–1992. They know the coffee has burned others in the past. McDonald's sells over 1.3 million cups a day.

Ms. Liebeck sues McDonald's. She asks McDonald's to pay for her medical costs and for her pain and suffering.

---

1. What are the facts in this case?

2. What reason will Ms. Liebeck use for filing a civil lawsuit?

3. What arguments will Ms. Liebeck's lawyer use to prove that Ms. Liebeck should receive money for medical costs, pain, and suffering?

4. What arguments will McDonald's use to prove that Ms. Liebeck should not win the lawsuit?

5. Do you think Ms. Liebeck should get any money from McDonald's? If so, how much?

6. What do you think is McDonald's responsibility to the community and to all the families that eat there?

LESSON 4

Solving Conflicts

After this lesson you will be able to:
- ➤ define and identify a conflict.
- ➤ list the steps in solving conflicts.
- ➤ choose which method of solving a conflict is best in a given situation.

WORDS TO KNOW

arguments – reasons for disagreement between two or more
  parties presented to a judge *(noun)*
pros – arguments in favor *(noun)*
cons – arguments in opposition *(noun)*

WHAT IS CONFLICT?

- What other words come to your mind when you hear the
  word *conflict*?
- What is your definition of conflict?
- How does conflict affect you?
- How do you react to conflict?

Conflicts or disputes often arise when two or more people have
different opinions on a subject. Both people think they are right. You
accidentally bump into someone in the hall and the person thinks it
was on purpose. You argue with your sister or brother. You turn the
stereo up too loud for your parents. These are conflicts. Conflict is a
part of everyday life. There will always be conflict in your life. The
question is, how do you handle conflict?

- Describe some conflicts that you have had recently.
- How did you and the other person involved handle the conflict?

WAYS TO SETTLE CONFLICT

There are many ways to settle everyday conflicts. Most people settle conflicts on their own without outside help. The people with a conflict talk to each other and work out their problem. Both sides want to
settle the dispute. This is the most frequent way people solve conflicts.

Sometimes people with a conflict fight. This usually turns out to
be a poor way to settle the conflict because, after the fight is over, the
conflict or problem is still there. Other times people with a conflict
separate so they can cool off. Cooling off keeps the conflict from
getting bigger, but it does not solve it. Many times, people who go
to cool off return later to talk.

Many times, people with a conflict go to someone else for help. The third person will either solve the problem directly or help the two people with a conflict talk about their problem and settle their differences. For example, Jeff is playing with a video game. He puts it down to help his mother in the kitchen. Beverly, his sister, comes along and starts to play with the same video game. When Jeff returns from the kitchen, he wants the game back. He says that he had it first. Jeff and Beverly go to their mother so she can decide who gets the game. The mother can either decide who gets the game or tell Jeff and Beverly to talk it out and come back and tell her their decision. Which way would you prefer?

Courts can help solve conflicts. When people with a conflict go to court, they agree to let a judge listen to their **arguments** and make a decision for them. The people with the conflict must follow the decision of the judge. There are sometimes disadvantages to going to court. Going to court can take a long time. It is also costly. Often the person who loses becomes angry and takes that anger out on the person with whom he or she had the conflict.

YOUR TURN 4-1

SETTLING DISPUTES

Read the following situations. List all of the ways that could be used to settle each dispute. Then decide the best method for solving the conflict. Give your reasons.

1. A landlord will not make needed repairs in an apartment because she thinks the people who live there caused the damage.

2. A used car stops running after two weeks and the dealer refuses to repair it.

3. There is one television. One brother wants to watch MTV and the other wants to watch the football game.

4. A married couple wants a divorce. The husband wants the two children to live with him, and the wife wants them to live with her.

5. Jerome invites Pam to the prom and pays for flowers, a tuxedo, and a limousine. Pam, who agreed to go, changes her mind and accepts an invitation from Miguel, instead.

SOLVING CONFLICTS

If you suggested that the people with the conflict talk to each other and work out the problem, you suggested the most frequent way people do solve conflicts. They talk to each other about their problem and try to reach an acceptable solution. While it is not always easy to solve conflicts by talking to the other person, you can learn to solve some conflicts by practicing.

Steps for Solving Conflicts

Step 1	*Define the problem.* Describe the problem. Do not describe the people who are involved.
Step 2	*Brainstorm solutions.* Think of as many ways to solve the problem as you can.
Step 3	*Consider what will happen.* Think of the **pros** and **cons** of each solution.
Step 4	*Choose and act on the most workable solution.* Choose the solution that seems best. Then act.
Step 5	*Try again.* If the first solution doesn't work, try another one.

YOUR TURN 4-2

SOLVING CONFLICTS STEP BY STEP

Look at the following situations. Use the steps for solving conflicts to settle each dispute.

A. Kareem and Mandla share a room. They disagree about how the room should be arranged.

B. Rachel accuses Li, who is not well liked, of stealing her money from the locker which they share. Rachel accuses Li loudly while she and Li are in the hall. Li denies taking the money.

C. Ken Lopez takes a new $100 sport coat to Ace Dry Cleaners to have it cleaned. Ken had only worn it a few times. When Ken picked it up, he found a large cigarette burn on the collar. Ken says the burn was not there when he took the coat to the cleaners. Ken also says he does not smoke. Ken asks the cleaners to pay him $100. Ace says its company is not responsible for the burn. Ace refuses to pay. Ace argues that the coat is used clothing and is no longer worth $100. Ken says he would have to pay at least $100 for a new coat.

D. Arnold is a cigarette smoker. He works in an insurance office with glass dividers. The dividers do not reach the ceiling. They are only five feet high. Twenty other employees have similar offices in the area near him. Arnold says he smokes because it is a habit he cannot break. He also says it reduces the stress of his job. Samantha's office is next to Arnold's. Samantha says that smoking is unhealthy for Arnold and for everyone else in the office. Samantha wants Arnold to stop smoking at work.

LESSON 5

Hiring a Lawyer

After this lesson you will be able to:

➤ tell what a lawyer does.
➤ explain how to find a lawyer.
➤ decide when you need to hire a lawyer.

WORDS TO KNOW

represent – to act or speak for *(verb)*

contract – an agreement *(noun)*

legal – dealing with the law *(adjective)*

manufacturer – someone who makes goods in large amounts *(noun)*

guarantee – a promise to replace something sold if it does not work or last as it should *(noun)*

income tax return – a form on which you write how much money you made and how much you owe in taxes to the government for the year *(noun)*

lawyer referral service – the name of a place to call to find a lawyer *(noun)*

clients – people who use a lawyer *(noun)*

appoint – to name or choose to represent you *(verb)*

Lawyers spend more time in an office than in a courtroom.

LAWYERS

What is a lawyer? A lawyer is also called an attorney or counselor. Lawyers are people trained to understand laws and the legal system. Lawyers can help:

- **represent** you in court.
- read a **contract**.
- give **legal** advice.

When you picture a lawyer, you may think of an older man in a three-piece suit. Today's lawyers can be old or young, male or female. Nearly half of all lawyers are under 35 years of age. The number of women lawyers has increased greatly in recent years.

A lawyer spends more time in an office than in a courtroom. Lawyers spend a lot of time studying and writing legal cases and papers. Sometimes lawyers help to settle a dispute so a person will not have to go to court.

DO YOU NEED A LAWYER?

Almost everything you do—from buying things, to driving a car, to talking with others—involves the law in some way. But you do not need a lawyer every time your activities involve the law. For example, if you disagree with a salesperson about returning a damaged radio, you may want to talk to the manager. If that doesn't work, you should contact the **manufacturer** or the Better Business Bureau. Your problem may be solved without going to a lawyer. There are times, however, when you need to talk to a lawyer. It is sometimes hard to tell when you should talk to a lawyer, but everyone agrees that you should hire a lawyer for major life events.

When to Hire a Lawyer

✔ If you are charged with a crime.

✔ If you start a business.

✔ If you get divorced.

✔ If you adopt a child.

✔ Before you make a will.

✔ Before you sign an important contract.

✔ If you are in an accident and someone is hurt or something is damaged.

Can you think of other times you might want to hire a lawyer?

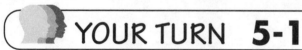 YOUR TURN 5-1

WOULD YOU HIRE A LAWYER?

Read the following cases and decide if you would hire a lawyer. Give your reasons.

1. You borrow a friend's car without telling her. She tells the police it was stolen. The police stop you and arrest you for stealing the car.

2. You buy a new stereo for $300. Three weeks later it breaks. You return it to the store. The salesperson says you cannot return it. Stereos have only a two-week **guarantee**.

3. You want to trade in your old car and buy a new one.

4. You apply for a job and are not hired. You think it is because you use a wheelchair.

5. You want to write a will.

6. You want to get a divorce.

7. You earned $5,000 working in a restaurant. You want to do your **income tax return**.

FINDING A LAWYER

How do you find a lawyer? A good place to look is in the telephone book's Yellow Pages. Look under the words "Lawyers," "**Lawyer Referral Service**," or "Legal Services." You can also ask your family or friends if they know a good lawyer. Be sure to find a lawyer who has experience with your kind of problem.

THE COST OF A LAWYER

Before going to the first meeting with a lawyer, it is important to ask if there is a fee. Some lawyers meet with you once without charging you any money, but others don't. The first meeting helps you decide if you want to hire that lawyer. Discuss the cost of the rest of your case at this time. Lawyers charge either by the hour, by the case, or by the amount won. Always ask for the fees in a written statement.

Many cities have legal aid or legal services programs. These programs offer free or low-cost legal services to those in need. Legal services programs accept **clients** based on how much money they earn, where they live, and the sizes of their families. Legal services offices handle cases like divorce, wills, and evictions. They do not accept cases of people accused of a crime.

If you are accused of a crime and cannot afford a lawyer, the judge may **appoint** a lawyer to defend you. If you use a court-appointed lawyer, there is often no fee or just a small fee.

◆ **FIGURE 5-1**   ADVICE FOR WORKING WITH A LAWYER

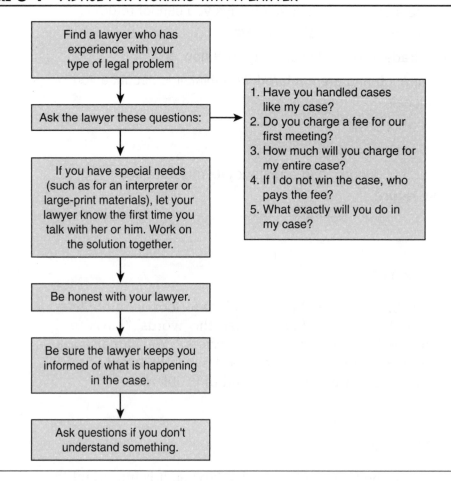

 **YOUR TURN 5-2**

MEETING WITH A LAWYER

1. Write questions a client would ask a lawyer and a lawyer would ask a client.
2. Role-play the first meeting between a client who wants a divorce and a lawyer.

Laws Protect Everyone

After this lesson you will be able to:
- ➤ explain the statement "all people are created equal."
- ➤ tell what is a civil rights law.
- ➤ define the term *disability*.
- ➤ give an example of a "reasonable accommodation."

 # WORDS TO KNOW

discrimination – unfair and unequal treatment *(noun)*

civil rights laws – laws that prevent others from taking away
something that is owed a person or a group of people *(noun)*

disability – a condition of not being able to do something *(noun)*

accent – a special way of pronouncing words *(noun)*

reject – refuse to take *(verb)*

physical – having to do with the body rather than the mind
(adjective)

mental – having to do with the mind *(adjective)*

public services – services provided for all people *(noun)*

qualified – having the skills that are needed *(adjective)*

accommodations – adjustments that meet a need *(noun)*

". . . no state shall . . . deny to any person . . . the equal protection of the laws."

LAWS PROTECT ALL PEOPLE

People differ in many ways. Some people are tall, and others are short. Some people are strong, while others are not. People have different skills and abilities. But in the United States, there is a basic belief that all people are to be given an equal chance to show what they can do. This belief was written into the Declaration of Independence in 1776. The Declaration of Independence uses these words to say the same thought: "All men are created equal." Today, when we read this statement, we mean "All people are created equal." "People" includes men and women. People who see, hear, get around, behave, speak, or learn differently are included, too. People of different races and religions as well as those from every country are also included.

How old must you be to get a driver's license in your state?

Since all people are created equal, everyone has the right to expect the government to treat them in the same way. If a person is treated differently, we say that he or she was discriminated against. Some kinds of **discrimination** are against the law. Discrimination means to treat a person or group of people differently from other people. For example, if a public school system only educates youth who are white, they discriminate against youth who are not white. That is against the law. Can you think of anyone who has been discriminated against?

All cases of discrimination are not against the law. For example, there are laws in every state that require a person to be a certain age to get a driver's license. These laws discriminate because they treat those below a certain age differently. This is age discrimination. However, this discrimination is legal. Discrimination, if it is reasonable, is not against the law. Most people consider it reasonable to think that people under 15 or 16 years old are too young to be responsible drivers. What do you think?

There are laws to protect the rights of people who feel they have not been treated fairly or who have been discriminated against. They are called **civil rights laws**. A civil right is something owed to a person that cannot be taken away. A civil rights law prevents a person or a group of people from taking away something that is owed to everyone. For example, there are civil rights laws that make it illegal for the owner of a restaurant to refuse to serve a person just because he or she is African American. There are civil rights laws that make it illegal to refuse to let a woman into law school just because she is a woman, and there are civil rights laws that make it illegal to refuse to hire a person who is in a wheelchair just because the person has a **disability**.

YOUR TURN 6-1

SHOULD THERE BE A CIVIL RIGHTS LAW?

Read each case and decide if there should be a law.

1. Carlos speaks Spanish at home with his parents. He wants to work in a bank. The bank manager will not hire him because he speaks English with an **accent**. Should there be a civil rights law that makes it illegal for the bank manager to refuse to hire Carlos? Give your reasons.

2. Ms. Spooner wants to be a teacher but did not go to college. The school will not hire her until she gets a college degree. Should there be a civil rights law that makes it illegal for the school to refuse to hire Ms. Spooner? Give your reasons.

3. Marlene is blind and wants to work in a grocery store. The store manager tells her she only hires people who can see. Should there be a law that makes it illegal for the store manager to refuse to hire people who are blind? Give your reasons.

4. Victor wants to be a nurse. The nursing school rejects him because it only allows women students. Should there be a law that makes it illegal for the school to **reject** Victor? Give your reasons.

5. Suzanne coaches the girls' soccer team. Fred coaches the boys' soccer team. Fred makes $10,000 more than Suzanne. Should there be a law that makes it against the law for Fred to be paid more than Suzanne for the same work? Give your reasons.

6. Joy, an Asian American, wants to rent an apartment. The landlord says no. He only rents to people who are white. Should there be a law that makes it illegal to rent only to people who are white? Give your reasons.

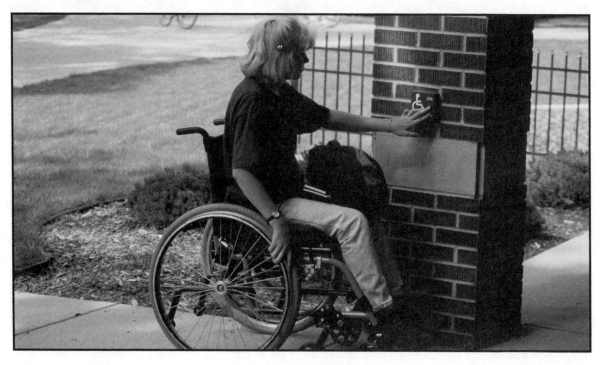

What is a disability?

PEOPLE WITH DISABILITIES

Over 43 million children, teens, and adults have disabilities. What is a disability? A disability is a difference in how people see, hear, get around, behave, work, speak, or learn. A disability is something **physical** or **mental** that affects everyday activities. For example, if you use a wheelchair, what everyday activity does that affect? If you cannot understand what you read as well as some of your friends, what everyday activity does that affect? A person with a disability has the same right as others to get a job, live in an apartment, call for a pizza, go shopping, see a doctor, or stay in a hotel.

There are civil rights laws that protect the rights of people with disabilities. One law is the Americans with Disabilities Act of 1990 (see Figure 6-1). Most people call the law the ADA. The ADA says that people with disabilities have the right to be treated the same as everyone else. It says that people and their abilities come before a person's disability. Basically, the ADA requires that businesses and governments make sure that jobs and **public services** are open to people with disabilities.

Fred wants to work as a store cashier. He is hard of hearing. The store will hire him if he can do the job. What is the job of a cashier? Would you hire Fred?

◆ **FIGURE 6-1**   AMERICANS WITH DISABILITIES ACT LEGISLATION

ADA is the acronym for the Americans with Disabilities Act of 1990, Public Law 101-336. The ADA has been called the most comprehensive antidiscrimination legislation since the Civil Rights Act of 1964. This federal legislation prohibits discrimination against qualified people with disabilities. The goal of the ADA is to bring people with disabilities into the economic and social mainstream of American life.

The ADA requires businesses, public entities, and state and local governments to provide reasonable accommodations to ensure that jobs and services are accessible to people with disabilities. Services and public accommodations covered by the ADA include any service or place that is provided for, or open to, the public.

Following is a list of the areas with which the ADA is concerned, along with the agency responsible for enforcement of each area:

- Title 1—Employment   Enforced by the Equal Employment
                                        Opportunity Commission (EEOC)

- Title 2—Public Services and   Enforced by the U.S. Department of
  Transportation   Justice

- Title 3—Public Accommodations   Enforced by the U.S. Department of
                                        Justice

- Title 4—Telecommunications   Enforced by the Federal Communications
                                        Commission (FCC)

- Title 5—Other miscellaneous
  areas

Complaints pertaining to noncompliance with the ADA can be filed by anyone, disabled or nondisabled. Complaints are filed with the appropriate agency, or with the Department of Justice, who then investigates the complaint. If the complaint is found to be valid, the organization may be given a specified amount of time to make the accommodation(s), and\or may be fined. A complaint is not a lawsuit, but citizens can file a private lawsuit.

The agencies involved encourage workers and employers to resolve disputes informally and internally whenever possible. The goal is to have people negotiate a solution themselves, if possible, without resorting to a formal complaint or lawsuit.

Why was the Americans with Disabilities Act passed?

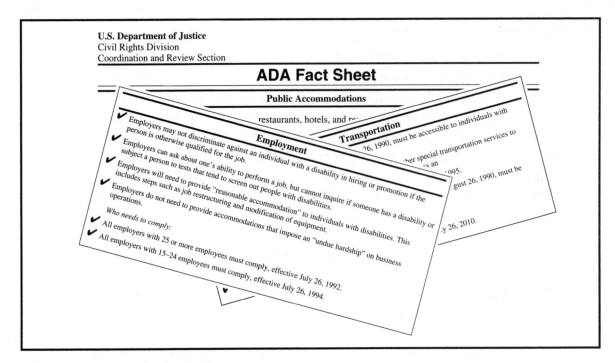

What areas are covered by the ADA?

The Americans with Disabilities Act states that:

1. State and local governments may not discriminate against a **qualified** person with a disability.

2. In hiring, employers may not discriminate against a person with a disability if the person is qualified for the job.

3. Restaurants, hotels, and stores may not discriminate against a person with a disability.

4. New public buses must be usable by a person with a disability.

5. Bus and train stations must be usable by a person with a disability.

6. Telephone companies must offer a special telephone service called a "telephone relay service." This service enables people with a speaking or hearing disability to use a telephone.

7. A new public place must be built so it is usable by a person with a disability.

EMPLOYERS MUST MAKE ACCOMMODATIONS

The ADA says that employers need to make "reasonable **accommodations**" for people with disabilities. An accommodation is an adjustment. It means to make something suitable. Examples of accommodations are a ramp, a sign language interpreter, or a large-print book. Accommodations make a job, a store, a bus, an apartment, or other places usable by everyone. Look around your building and locate an accommodation made there. What type of disability is accommodated?

The person with a disability *must ask* for things he or she needs. The employer does not have to provide an accommodation if the employee does not ask for it. An accommodation should not cause the employer's business to suffer.

June works as a secretary. She needs her desk a little higher so her wheelchair will fit under it. June asked her boss to raise the desk. A raised desk is her accommodation.

YOUR TURN 6-2

MAKING ACCOMMODATIONS

Read the cases below. Decide what accommodation each person should ask for.

1. Michael has tickets to a professional football game with his friends. He uses a wheelchair. Michael wants to sit with his friends in the bleachers.

   a. Does Michael have a disability?
   b. What is Michael's disability?
   c. List the things Michael must consider before attending the game.
   d. If Michael asks for an accommodation, what would it be?
   e. Whom will Michael ask for the accommodation?
   f. When should Michael ask for the accommodation?
   g. Must the person Michael asks provide the accommodation? Give your reasons.

2. Gina is a high school student who is enrolled in classes for students with learning disabilities. She wants to apply for a part-time job as a cashier at a fast-food restaurant. Gina thinks she must take a math test before she can be hired. She thinks she can pass it if she takes her time.

   a. Does Gina have a disability?
   b. What is Gina's disability?
   c. List the things Gina must consider before applying for the job.
   d. If Gina asks for an accommodation, what would it be?
   e. Whom will Gina ask for the accommodation?
   f. When should Gina ask for the accommodation?
   g. Must the person Gina asks provide the accommodation? Give your reasons.

LESSON 7

Crime

After this lesson you will be able to:
- ➤ define crime, felony, and misdemeanor.
- ➤ explain the difference between a felony and a misdemeanor.
- ➤ list some crimes that are felonies.
- ➤ list some crimes that are misdemeanors.

WORDS TO KNOW

crime – an act that one does or doesn't do that breaks the law (*noun*)

legislature – a group of people with the power to make and change laws (*noun*)

concealed – hidden or kept out of sight (*adjective*)

probation – a time period when a person convicted of a crime is allowed to stay out of jail; someone supervises the person (*noun*)

politician – a person who is elected to a government office (*noun*)

bribe – money given to a person in order to influence his or her actions (*noun*)

felonies – crimes for which the punishment may be one year or more in prison; a felony is more serious than a misdemeanor (*noun*)

misdemeanors – crimes for which the punishment may be less than one year in prison; a misdemeanor is less serious than a felony (*noun*)

simple assault – use of force or a physical attack that is not serious (*noun*)

traffic violations – actions which break laws concerning the vehicles or people moving along a route (*noun*)

CRIME

What's a **crime**? Did you say murder, rape, shoplifting, or robbery? These are all crimes. Crimes are acts that break the law. The job of a state **legislature** is to make laws. Legislatures decide which acts are crimes and which are not crimes. Legislatures sometimes disagree over which acts should or should not be crimes. For example, the Michigan state legislature decided that in Michigan carrying a **concealed** handgun without a license is a crime, but the Texas legislature decided that it is *not* a crime to carry a concealed handgun without a license in Texas. Legislatures decide which acts are crimes based on what most people believe is right. Certain acts are not

What crimes might be stopped by neighborhood crime watchers?

allowed in order to protect life and property, to keep order, and to protect people's rights.

People who commit crimes may be punished. That punishment may be a fine, jail, **probation,** or something else. A person who commits a crime is called a criminal. A criminal can be anyone. He or she can be a parent who beats a child, a thief who steals a car, a drunk driver who kills someone, a businessperson who steals money through use of a computer, or a **politician** who takes a **bribe.** Criminals may be any race: white, African American, Asian American, Native American, or Latino. They may be young or old, male or female. They may be poor or rich.

YOUR TURN 7-1

THE BANK ROBBERY

Read this story. Which actions in this story do you think
are crimes?

Carlos and Jason plan to rob the First National Bank. They need
the money to pay their bills. They do not want to injure anyone so
Jason gets a high-powered water gun. He plans to keep the gun in
his coat so that its shape will frighten the bank teller. Carlos
volunteers to drive the getaway car, a new yellow Ford. They plan
the robbery at a time when the bank has few customers.

Just before leaving to rob the bank, Jason gets a call from his
girlfriend, Kathy. Now they are late. Carlos makes up for lost time by
speeding and running red lights.

Unfortunately, they hit a woman in a crosswalk and don't stop to
help her. The woman later dies.

At the bank, Jason notices that the water gun has leaked,
soaking the front of his coat. They consider calling off the robbery
but decide to go ahead. Everything goes smoothly, until the teller
sets off the alarm as Jason runs from the bank.

Thinking quickly, Carlos and Jason leave their car and jump into
a new Corvette. (The owner carelessly left the keys in the car.) They
leave town and later sell the Corvette to Honest Harvey's Used Car
Sales for $1,000 without a title.

With the water gun and the money from the bank robbery,
Carlos and Jason walk toward Kathy's house. As they cross the
street, they ignore a "Don't Walk" sign. A police officer stops them,
sees the money and the gun, and arrests them.

 YOUR TURN **7-2**

NAME THAT CRIME

Read "The Bank Robbery" again.

1. List the names of all the crimes that were committed.

2. How many crimes did you list?

3. Compare your list with the teacher's.

Name some crimes that should be misdemeanors.

FELONIES AND MISDEMEANORS

There are two groups of crimes. They are **felonies** and **misdemeanors**. A felony is more serious than a misdemeanor. A felony is a crime punishable by one year or more in prison. Some felonies may be punishable by death. Carjacking, murder, rape, and drug dealing are all felonies. People convicted of a felony will lose certain rights. They will lose the right to vote and the right to serve on a jury. They cannot join any military service. Also, convicted felons may not work as doctors, lawyers, or teachers. Why do you think this is so?

Misdemeanors are less serious crimes. A misdemeanor is a crime for which the punishment may be less than one year in prison. People convicted of misdemeanors will not lose their rights as do convicted felons. **Simple assault**, shoplifting something that costs less than $100, and hitting someone with your fist are misdemeanors. Minor **traffic violations** are not misdemeanors or crimes, although they are punishable by law.

YOUR TURN 7-3

FELONY VERSUS MISDEMEANOR

Following is a list of crimes. Decide if you think the crime *should* be a felony or a misdemeanor. Give your reasons.

1. Stealing a parked car.
2. Spray painting the doors of a school.
3. Selling a small amount of crack cocaine.
4. Buying a small amount of crack cocaine.
5. Cheating on your tax return so you get back $500 instead of paying $200.
6. Shoplifting a pair of jeans.
7. Shooting the person who killed your brother.
8. Driving while you are drunk.

YOUR TURN 7-4

UNDERSTANDING LEGISLATURES' REASONS

Review your notes that list the reasons crimes are misdemeanors or felonies. Based on your list and what you read, tell the reasons legislatures might decide to make some crimes misdemeanors and others felonies.

1. The reason some crimes are misdemeanors is that:

2. The reason some crimes are felonies is that:

LESSON 8

Crime Victims

After this lesson you will be able to:

➤ identify the most frequent victims of crime.
➤ give advice on how to report a crime.
➤ decide when to report a crime.

WORDS TO KNOW

imagine – to make up a picture or idea in the mind *(verb)*

victims – people who are hurt, suffer a loss, or are killed *(noun)*

violent – showing or acting with great force that causes damage or injury *(adjective)*

aggravated assault – a very serious use of force or a physical attack *(noun)*

city – a large town; a place where many people and businesses are located *(noun)*

suburbs – places that are near the outskirts of a city *(noun)*

rural – having to do with the country or the people who live there *(adjective)*

suspects – people someone thinks of as probably guilty of some wrong action *(noun)*

TEENS ARE VICTIMS

Shoplifting! Robbery! Theft! Crime affects everyone. Especially teens. How many people are there in your school? **Imagine** there are 1,000 teens. Of every 1,000 teens, 67 of them will be **victims** of **violent** crime this year. If you had 1,000 adults, only 26 of them would be victims of violent crime this year. Teens are far more likely than adults to be victims of violent crime.

How many of these people will be victims of a violent crime?

TABLE 1

Kinds of Violent Crimes (for every 1,000 people)			
	Victims 12–15 years	Victims 16–19 years	Adult Victims
Rape	9	23	6
Robbery	92	100	48
Aggravated assault	131	222	72
Simple assault (fighting)	383	379	134
TOTAL VIOLENT CRIMES FOR EVERY 1,000 PEOPLE	616	724	260

Source: *U.S. Department of Justice, Bureau of Justice Statistics*, A National Crime Survey Report, *May 1991: NCJ-128129.*

TABLE 2

Victims of Violent Crimes (for every 1,000 people)		
	Victims 12–15 years	Victims 16–19 years
Sex:		
Male	782	934
Female	441	512
Race:		
White	605	720
African American	692	748
Other	535	704

Source: *U.S. Department of Justice, Bureau of Justice Statistics*, A National Crime Survey Report, *May 1991: NCJ-128129.*

TABLE 3

Locations of Violent Crimes (for every 1,000 people)		
	Victims 12–15 years	Victims 16–19 years
City	797	892
Suburbs	567	681
Rural	518	613

Source: *U.S. Department of Justice, Bureau of Justice Statistics*, A National Crime Survey Report, *May 1991: NCJ-128129.*

YOUR TURN 8-1

CRIMES OF VIOLENCE

Use the data in Tables 1, 2, and 3 to tell whether these statements are true or false. Write the answers on a separate piece of paper.

1. Teens aged 12–15 are less likely to be victims of violent crime than are teens who are 16–19 years old.

2. More teens 16–19 years old get raped than adults.

3. More adults get robbed than children 12–15 years old.

4. Fewer males 16–19 years old are victims of violent crime than are females 16–19 years old.

5. More males 12–15 years old are victims of violent crime than females 12–15 years old.

6. African American males aged 16–19 years are more likely victims of violent crime than white males aged 16–19.

7. Teens who live in the city are safer than teens who live anywhere else.

REPORTING CRIME

Even though teens are more likely to be victims of crime, they are less likely to report crime. Why do you think this is so? Have you ever been the victim of a crime? If you are ever a victim of or a witness to a crime, you should do the following:

If You Are a Crime Victim

✔ Stay calm.

✔ Call the police immediately.

✔ Tell the police:

    1. who you are.

    2. where you are.

    3. what happened, briefly.

✔ If anyone is hurt, ask for an ambulance.

✔ When the police arrive, tell them exactly what you saw. Try to remember things like:

    1. who committed the crime.

    2. how many **suspects** there are.

    3. age, sex, race, height, and weight of the suspects.

    4. what the suspects were wearing.

    5. car license number or other important information.

 YOUR TURN **8-2**

WHAT WOULD YOU DO?

1. Read each case and answer these questions about each one.

   • What would you do?
   • Would you report the case to the police?
   • Why or why not?

   a. One night you see two teens throwing rocks. They break 20 windows of your high school.

   b. One afternoon at 2:30 P.M., you see a green van pull up in front of a neighbor's house. Two strange men get out of the van and walk to the back of the house. You know your neighbors are on vacation.

Your Turn 8-2 (continued)

c. One day, at lunchtime, you see a blue car slow down near a group of teens who go to your school. Suddenly, you see someone in the car point a gun and shoot at the group. You get a good look at the shooter and the car.

2. Pick one case to report. Role-play a pretend phone call between you and the police. Let one person report the crime and pretend to be the police dispatcher who receives the call. Tape-record or videotape the role-play.

 # YOUR TURN 8-3

THE KITTY GENOVESE STORY

Listen to your teacher read a case about a victim. Take notes. Be prepared to answer these questions:

1. Who is the victim?

2. Where did the story take place?

3. When did it happen?

4. What happened?

5. What is the main idea of the story?

6. How could Kitty's life have been saved?

7. Why do you think people did not call the police?

Driving and Alcohol

After this lesson you will be able to:

➤ define drunk driving.
➤ discuss what can happen when people drink and drive.
➤ suggest actions to take when offered a ride with a drunk driver.

 **WORDS TO KNOW**

under the influence – affected by something such as drugs or
   alcohol *(adjective)*

drunk driver – someone whose driving is affected by alcohol or
   drugs *(noun)*

intoxicated – drunk *(adjective)*

average – not out of the ordinary *(adjective)*

consequences – results of an action *(noun)*

investigate – to look at or study carefully *(verb)*

 YOUR TURN **9-1**

HIGH SCHOOL STUDENTS, DRINKING, AND DRIVING

Look at the pie charts and answer these questions.

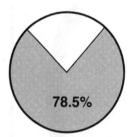

Percentage who have
ridden with a drunk driver

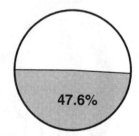

Percentage of drivers
who have driven while drunk

1. What percentage of students ride in a car with a driver who is
   drunk or **under the influence** of alcohol or drugs?
2. What percentage of students drive while under the influence of
   alcohol or drugs?

DRUNK DRIVERS

A **drunk driver** is someone whose driving is affected by alcohol or drugs. Sometimes police call a drunk driver someone who is driving while **intoxicated** (DWI) or driving under the influence (DUI). What do the police call a drunk driver in your state?

Can you tell when someone is drunk? Every state has tests that tell whether a person charged with DUI or DWI is legally drunk. These

Would you allow your 18-year-old daughter to attend a New Year's Eve party?

tests tell how much alcohol there is in your blood. In most states, a man who is **average** weight and drinks more than one drink an hour, for up to three hours, is considered drunk. Many times this is different from the everyday definition of drunk. A person does not have to stagger before being considered drunk according to the law.

Riding in a car with a drunk driver can result in serious **consequences**. There are 22,500 highway deaths a year. In 1991, 5,749 of these were teenage deaths. One-half of the teenage deaths involved alcohol. Additionally, thousands of teens were injured in highway accidents. If you were a state legislator, what laws would you pass to reduce the number of teen deaths involving alcohol?

 YOUR TURN **9-2**

THE INVESTIGATION

Read the following story. Pretend you are a police officer assigned to **investigate** this accident. You uncovered some facts, but you need to learn more. Decide to whom you should talk to find the facts listed below.

WHEN ALCOHOL KILLS

Mr. and Mrs. Thompson have an 18-year-old daughter, who is a high school senior, named Jane. On December 31, Jane kissed her parents goodnight before leaving for a New Year's Eve party with Satch, her date. Her father told her to be home by 1:00 A.M. She said, "Dad, it's a special night, let me stay out later. We will be at Curt's house and it is my last New Year's together with all my friends." Since Jane had always been a responsible daughter and a good driver, her Dad gave in and told her to be home by 2:00 A.M.

Mr. and Mrs. Thompson had a quiet New Year's Eve at home. They went to bed around 10:00 P.M. They were in bed waiting for Jane to come home when they received a phone call from Curt's mother. She asked if Jane was home. Mr. Thompson said no. She said that there had been an accident on Main Street. Mr. Thompson and his wife hurriedly dressed and drove to the crash site, less than a mile from their home.

They parked at the top of the hill and walked over to a police officer on the scene and asked if Jane was in the accident. The officer said yes. They asked if she was alive. The officer said no. Thinking it was a bad dream, they followed the ambulance to the hospital. When Mr. Thompson saw Jane, he realized that it wasn't a bad dream. She was dead and there was nothing they could do to bring her back.

At first no one had all the facts. The police investigation found that a lot of people had not acted responsibly. If only one of the people that Jane saw that day had been more responsible, Jane might still be alive.

1. It was a single-car accident.

2. The driver was Satch.

3. Satch had been drinking.

4. Jane was riding with Satch.

5. Curt's parents were upstairs during the party.

6. Curt served beer at the party.

PREVENTING DRUNK DRIVING

There are state laws that try to lower the number of teen traffic deaths. Some states have youth-driving curfew laws. These laws allow teens to drive only between certain hours. Usually, the teen driver is not allowed to drive after midnight. Also, at least 15 states have a different definition of the term *drunk* for drivers younger than 21.

Many communities that are concerned about drinking and driving start community prevention programs. Mothers against Drunk Drivers (MADD) is a program that fights for stricter DUI laws. MADD works to make people aware of the dangers of drunk driving.

YOUR TURN 9-3

PREVENTING DRUNK DRIVING

Read the questions which follow. Decide the places you should call or visit to answer the questions.

1. Are there other programs to warn people about the dangers of drunk drivers?

2. How do people in your community find out about these programs?

3. Does your community have "call for a ride" programs?

4. Is there a Students against Drunk Drivers (SADD) club in your school?

LESSON 10

Date Rape

After this lesson you will be able to:

➤ define date rape.
➤ discuss a cause of rape.
➤ give advice about what to do if you are a rape victim.

WORDS TO KNOW

skydiving – the sport of jumping from an airplane and falling
   freely for some time before opening a parachute *(noun)*

instructor – teacher *(noun)*

date rape – the crime of forcing a person one knows to submit to
   sex *(noun)*

guilt – the feeling of having done something wrong *(noun)*

expert – a person who has great knowledge or skill in a certain
   area *(noun)*

YOUR TURN **10-1**

THE JUMP

Read this story. Discuss the questions which follow.

THE SKYDIVER

Bob lives in a community where **skydiving** is a popular sport. All of Bob's friends skydive. Bob wants to be a considered a "real man," so he saves money for skydiving lessons. He attends four classroom lessons. It is finally time for his first jump. Bob tells the **instructor** he is not sure he can jump, but wants to go on the flight. He puts on his skydiving equipment.

The plane is flying 7,000 feet above the ground. Bob peeps out of the open doorway. The wind whips against his face. His turn to jump comes, but he freezes, unable to move. Bob is scared. He wants to jump—everyone else is doing it. However, he knows it's not right for him.

Bob tells the instructor that he isn't going to jump.

Suddenly, the instructor pushes Bob out of the plane. Bob lands safely, but he is angry and shocked. He knows that he will never jump again.

1. What happened in the story?
2. Does Bob have the right to refuse to jump? Give your reasons.
3. Did Bob ever make the instructor think that he wanted to jump?
4. Was the instructor right or wrong to push Bob? Why?
5. What should Bob have done?

 YOUR TURN **10-2**

TONY AND JANE

Read the following story. Answer the questions at the end of the story.

TONY AND JANE

Tony attends high school. His friends like to talk about sex. He knows all of the "real men" are having sex. He wants to be part of that crowd.

One night, Tony invites Jane to a movie. Afterward, he invites her to his house. Tony tells Jane that his parents aren't home. Jane goes anyway. She just wants to relax, hear some music, and talk. Tony kisses Jane and asks her to make love. Jane tells Tony, no. She likes Tony, but she's scared. She knows this is not right for her. Suddenly, Tony pushes Jane onto the bed and forces her to have sex. Jane cries. She feels angry, helpless, and ashamed. Later, she refuses to go out with Tony again. She doesn't know if she should report it to the police. She feels partly responsible and doesn't know if she was raped or not.

1. Does Jane have the right to refuse to have sex? Why or why not?
2. Why did Tony force Jane to have sex?
3. Did Jane do anything to make Tony think that she wanted to have sex?
4. Was Tony right or wrong to force Jane?
5. Do you think Jane was raped?
6. What do you think Jane should do?
7. What should Tony do?

WHAT IS DATE RAPE?

Rape means using force to have sex against the victim's will. Some rapes are committed by strangers. However, most rapes are committed by someone who knows the victim. **Date rape** is the crime of using force to have sex, against the victim's will, when the rapist and the victim know each other.

No one knows how many people are victims of date rape each year. We do know that rape happens more often to teenage girls and young women than to older women or to men. Many date rape cases are never reported to the police. Victims who know their rapists are less likely to report the crime than those raped by strangers. Why do you think that is so? Sometimes the victim does not even think the attack was a rape. The law sees no difference between rape by strangers and rape by someone you know. Rape is rape, even if the attacker and victim know each other.

Why is date rape reported less often than stranger rape?

THE EFFECTS OF DATE RAPE

Most date rape victims feel anger, **guilt**, fear, and helplessness after an attack. They often blame themselves and wonder if something they said, did, or wore caused the attack. Usually the victim feels ashamed because she knew and trusted the rapist. These feelings make it hard for the victim to trust others.

CAUSES OF DATE RAPE

Sometimes rape happens when men and women mistakenly think they should act a certain way on a date. Some men believe that using force on a date is okay. They think, "Even if she says no, she means yes." Sometimes a woman believes that if the man buys her dinner, or pays for a movie or drinks, she owes him sex. Neither of these beliefs is true.

EXPERT ADVICE

It is never right to touch a person sexually if the person doesn't want you to. It is never okay to force sex. It is a crime. No person has the right to force or demand sex from another.

Some people believe that if a man pays for an expensive dinner, the woman owes the man sex. Do you think this is so?

It is important for dates to talk to each other about what they wish to do or not do before any action is taken.

Does your community have services for rape victims? Where would you try to find these services?

 **YOUR TURN 10-3**

HELP FOR THE VICTIM OF DATE RAPE

1. Use the telephone book to locate the address and phone number of the places where a rape victim can get services.
2. Write a list of questions about date rape that you would ask an **expert**.
3. Assume you are a writer for the school newspaper. Write an article telling other teens about date rape. Give them advice about how to avoid date rape and what to do if they become victims of date rape.

LESSON 11

The Arrest

After this lesson you will be able to:

➤ describe the arrest procedure.

➤ define the terms *stop*, *frisk*, *search*, and *arrest*.

➤ explain the Miranda rights, using your own words.

➤ list some rights and responsibilities juveniles have when arrested.

WORDS TO KNOW

disturbance – a lot of noise that interrupts the peace *(noun)*

uniformed – wearing an official police uniform *(adjective)*

reveals – uncovers; opens up to view *(verb)*

Miranda rights – the rights that must be explained before an arrested person can be questioned *(noun)*

mental retardation – an abnormal slowness of thought, development, or progress *(noun)*

possessions – things that a person owns; personal property *(noun)*

procedure – the rules and methods of carrying out a legal action *(noun)*

IS IT A STOP OR AN ARREST?

THE ARREST

STOP AND FRISK

John and his friend, Megan, go downtown on a dull Saturday afternoon. It is the week before Christmas and the downtown stores and streets are crowded. While you are walking along Main Street you suddenly see a **disturbance**. John and Megan run toward you. A woman chases them shouting, "Stop them, stop them! They have my purse!" You see John drop a purse and continue to run. A few seconds later, several **uniformed** police officers appear from the crowd. They chase John and Megan. When the police get close to the two young people, they shout, "Stop! Police! Don't move!" John and Megan stop right away. The police officers tell them, "Get on your knees. Put your hands behind your head." The officers then frisk John and Megan to look for weapons. The frisk **reveals** no weapons. The officers ask each of the young people to give his or her name, age, address, and telephone number. They also ask John and Megan why they are running.

YOUR TURN 11-1

STOP AND FRISK

Answer these questions about the story:

1. Did the police officers have a good reason to stop John and Megan? Give your reasons.
2. Did the police follow correct police procedure by stopping John and Megan?
3. Do you think John and Megan are required by law to give their names, ages, phone numbers, and addresses?
4. Should John and Megan give the officers their correct names, ages, phone numbers, and addresses?
5. Do you think the officers have the right to ask John and Megan why they are running?
6. Would you tell John and Megan to answer every question the police ask? Give your reason.

Would you answer all questions that a police officer asks?

The police stopped John and Megan; then they frisked them. A police stop is a brief question-and-answer period. It usually occurs when a police officer believes that something is suspicious. A police stop is not the same as an arrest. The police stop and question many people daily. However, they don't arrest everyone they stop. During a police stop, the person who is stopped is free to leave the area. This is not true of a police arrest. Sometimes, after a police stop, the police will frisk the person who is stopped. A frisk occurs when the police pat down a person's outer clothing. The purpose of a frisk is to check for weapons. A frisk is not the same as a search. A police officer will search the inside of a person's clothing, such as his or her pockets, if the officer suspects that the person has an illegal item. A search takes place after a frisk.

 YOUR TURN **11-2**

DEFINE THE TERM

1. Role-play these terms:

    a. A police stop

    b. An arrest

2. Explain the difference between these terms:

    a. A frisk

    b. A search (of a person)

THE ARREST (continued)

RIGHTS OF THE ARRESTED

Both John and Megan tell the officers their names, ages, addresses, and telephone numbers. John is 16 years old and Megan is 15 years old. They refuse to say why they were running. The woman identifies John as the purse snatcher. The police place John and Megan under arrest. The officers say, "You are under arrest," but they do not ask any more questions. They do not read John and Megan their **Miranda rights**. The officers then take the two young people to the police station.

YOUR TURN 11-3

RIGHTS OF THE ARRESTED

Discuss the following questions:

1. What rights do you think people have during an arrest?
2. Do you think the police did anything illegal by not reading John and Megan their Miranda rights at the time of their arrest?

ADMONITION AND WAIVER OF RIGHTS	AMONESTACION Y RENUNCIA DE DERECHOS
1. You have the right to remain silent. Do you understand?	1. Usted tiene el derecho de no hablar. Entiende?
2. Anything you say may be used against you in court. Do you understand?	2. Lo que usted diga podrá ser usado contra usted en la corte. Entiende?
3. You have the right to an attorney during questioning. Do you understand?	3. Usted tiene el derecho de tener un abogado aquí presente mientras que hablamos. Entiende?
4. If you cannot afford an attorney, one will be appointed for you, before any questioning. Do you understand?	4. Si quiere un abogado, pero no tiene dinero, la corte le dará uno antes de que hablemos. Entiende?

Why are some Miranda cards written in Spanish?

YOUR MIRANDA RIGHTS

The Fifth Amendment to the U.S. Constitution says that no one shall be forced to be a witness against himself or herself in a criminal case. This means you cannot be forced to confess in a police station or at a trial. In 1966, there was a criminal case called *Miranda versus Arizona.* Ernesto Miranda was accused of the kidnap and rape of an 18-year-old woman. He suffered from mild **mental retardation**. Miranda was picked from a police lineup by the victim. He was questioned for two hours and not told about his rights. Miranda confessed and was found guilty in the state of Arizona. Miranda's lawyer went to the Supreme Court to ask the court to strike down Miranda's guilty conviction. The lawyer said that the Fifth Amendment to the U.S. Constitution requires suspects to be told of their rights before they are questioned. Since Miranda was not told about his rights, he should not have been found guilty. The Supreme Court agreed with the lawyer and struck down the guilty conviction. Since this case, the practice we know today as "being read your rights" is also called "being given your Miranda rights."

Miranda rights must be explained before an arrested person can be questioned. The police do not have to read a person his or her rights before, or after, an arrest. This fact is often misunderstood. Many people falsely believe they must be read their rights immediately after an arrest. Whenever you see people being arrested on television, you see the police read the Miranda rights immediately after the arrest. While this is a common police practice, it is not required. Police are only required to read you your rights before questioning you.

The police must tell the person the Miranda rights in a way he or she can clearly understand. For example, if you cannot read, the Miranda rights must be read to you, or if you speak only Spanish, the information must be given in Spanish. The Miranda rights are listed below.

1. You have the right to remain silent. Anything you say can be used against you in court.
2. You have the right to a lawyer and to have one present while you are being questioned.
3. If you cannot afford a lawyer, one will be appointed for you before any questioning begins.

 YOUR TURN 11-4

MIRANDA RIGHTS

Answer these questions:

1. Explain the Miranda rights using your own words.
2. Give some reasons why police might read arrested people their rights, even before questioning them.

THE ARREST *(continued)*

THE STATION

Several things happen at the police station. The police officers search John and Megan. Next, the officers ask John and Megan for their parents' names and telephone numbers. The police call their parents. John and Megan are not allowed to make the telephone calls themselves. The officers do not try to question the two juveniles because neither a lawyer nor their parents are at the station. John and Megan are fingerprinted and photographed. In addition, the police officers take all of their money and personal **possessions**. The officers give receipts to John and Megan and ask for their signatures. John and Megan sign the receipts. The arrest **procedure** is completed.

END OF STORY

 YOUR TURN **11-5**

THE ARREST

Answer these questions:

1. Why did the police arrest John and Megan? What is the charge?
2. Whom would you call if you were given one phone call? Why?

POLICE STATION
731

JUVENILE RIGHTS

In most states a juvenile is anyone under the age of 17. Juveniles have the right to be treated with respect. Courts have guaranteed juveniles these rights:

1. Juveniles must be informed of their rights when they are placed under arrest.
2. Juveniles must be informed of the charges against them.
3. Parents must be informed of their child's arrest, the charges, and the place where the young person is being held.

JUVENILE RESPONSIBILITIES

Young people are responsible for their behavior. Think about John's and Megan's behavior. Did they do anything that was irresponsible? How did they act when the police officers stopped them? If you were one of the police officers, would you detain the juveniles or let them go home with their parents? What reasons can you give for releasing them?

Do you agree with the following list? What would you change or add to it?

How to Act If You Are Arrested

✔ Be polite to the officer.
✔ Tell the truth about your name, age, address, and telephone number.
✔ Don't run, fight, or curse.
✔ Do not make any statements about the charges or arrest without talking to your parents or a lawyer.
✔ Request a phone call to a parent or guardian and a lawyer.

LESSON 12

Juveniles' Rights

After this lesson you will be able to:

➤ define the terms *juvenile, delinquent,* and *due process.*

➤ tell some rights delinquent juveniles have in court.

➤ list differences between the juvenile court system and the adult court system.

 **WORDS TO KNOW**

delinquent – offending by neglect of duty or violation of duty or of law *(adjective)*

testimony – a solemn declaration made usually verbally by a witness under oath in response to questioning by a lawyer or authorized public official *(noun)*

appealed – made an earnest request *(verb)*

due process – fair treatment for anyone in the court system *(noun)*

testify – to talk about the case, under oath, in a court of law *(verb)*

hearing – a session in which witnesses are heard and testimony is taken *(noun)*

public – the people as a whole *(noun)*

rehabilitate – to restore to a former state *(verb)*

JUVENILES HAVE A SPECIAL COURT

A juvenile is any young person who is not legally an adult. State laws set the age limit for juveniles. In most states a juvenile is anyone under the age of 18.

Young people, or juveniles, are seldom treated the same as adults. Name a right an adult in your house has that a juvenile does not have. Some say that the reason adults have more rights than juveniles is that adults have more responsibilities than juveniles. Do you agree? Name one responsibility that an adult has that most juveniles don't have.

Our criminal justice system has special courts and procedures for juveniles who get into trouble with the law. Juvenile court is based on the idea that the court acts as a child's parent to protect and help the child. Therefore, there is no need for the juvenile court to pay close attention to formal procedures or rights. A juvenile who is found by the court to have broken a law is called **delinquent**.

Do you agree or disagree with the statement, "Juveniles in trouble should be helped, not punished"? Give your reasons.

THE COURT CASE OF GERALD GAULT

A neighbor, Mrs. Cook, accused Gerald Gault, aged 15, of making an obscene phone call. Making an obscene phone call is illegal. The police picked up Gerald and took him to the juvenile detention center. Gerald's mother was at work at the time. The police did not call to tell her what had happened to her son. Upon her return from work, Mrs. Gault looked for Gerald, but couldn't find him. Later that night, the police called Mrs. Gault and told her that they had Gerald and that there was a hearing the next day. Mrs. Gault was not told what the complaint was against Gerald.

The next day, at the hearing, a police officer testified that Mrs. Cook had said that Gerald made an obscene phone call to her. Mrs. Cook told the police that she recognized Gerald's voice. Mrs. Cook was not required to come to court. Gerald said he did not make the obscene remarks. Gerald blamed the call on a friend. There were no lawyers present. No one wrote down the court **testimony**. Therefore, there is no way of proving what anyone said at the hearing.

A judge heard the case. There is no jury in juvenile court. The judge said that Gerald was a delinquent and ordered Gerald to go to a state reform school. Gerald could stay there until he is 21 years old. An adult found guilty of the same crime could be sent to county jail for no longer than 60 days.

 YOUR TURN **12-1**

THE CASE OF GERALD GAULT

Was Gerald treated fairly or unfairly? Make two columns on a sheet of paper and list the fair and unfair events that happened to Gerald Gault.

Fair	Unfair
1. There was a judge at Gerald's hearing.	1. The police did not tell Gerald's mother that they had Gerald until late.

THE U.S. SUPREME COURT DECIDES

The case of Gerald Gault is an actual case that happened in 1967. At that time, even though there was a separate juvenile court, juveniles who went to court did not have the same rights as adults who went to court. Gerald's mother felt that this was unfair. She **appealed** the judge's decision until the case was heard in the U.S. Supreme Court. An appeal happens when you take a case to a court which has the power to change the decision of the other court. Mrs. Gault said that Gerald had been treated unfairly. She said that Gerald had not been given **due process**. Due process means fair treatment. The U.S. Supreme Court agreed with Mrs. Gault. They decided that Gerald Gault did not have due process of law. The Supreme Court said that the U.S. Constitution guarantees that a person's life, liberty, or property cannot be taken away without due process of law. Because of this case, juveniles are given due process rights in a juvenile court today.

Rights of a Juvenile Accused of a Crime

1. The right to notice of charges: A juvenile and his or her family must be told what the charge is against the juvenile. There should be enough time before the hearing to allow the juvenile, the family, and the lawyer to prepare their case.

2. The right to a lawyer: A juvenile has the right to a lawyer. If the juvenile does not have enough money to pay a lawyer, the court must appoint one.

3. The right to face your accuser: A juvenile must be allowed to hear the testimony of the witnesses and the accusers. The juvenile's lawyer must have a chance to ask witnesses questions.

4. The right to refuse to **testify** against themselves: Juveniles have the right to refuse to answer a question or give testimony against themselves. They must be told they have a right to remain silent because anything they say may be used against them.

Do you think there should be a jury in juvenile court? Give your reason.

THE DIFFERENCE BETWEEN JUVENILE AND ADULT COURT

If a juvenile gets into trouble with the law, a court system is already set up to handle only juvenile cases. Juvenile court is based on the idea that children in trouble with the law should be helped,

Juvenile Court	Adult Criminal Court
1. A juvenile is usually under 18 years of age.	1. An adult is usually 18 years of age or older.
2. An illegal act which is committed by a juvenile is called an offense.	2. An illegal act which is committed by an adult is called a crime.
3. In juvenile court, the proceedings held by the judge are called a **hearing**.	3. In adult criminal court, the proceedings held by the judge are called a trial.
4. A juvenile can be taken to court for a. truancy from school b. failure to obey parents c. running away from home	4. An adult *cannot* be taken to court for a. truancy from school b. failure to obey parents c. running away from home
5. A juvenile has a hearing that is private and confidential. The **public** is not allowed to come to watch it.	5. An adult has a trial that is public. Anyone can come to watch it.
6. A juvenile does not have the right to a jury.	6. An adult has the right to a jury.
7. A judge in juvenile court considers the juvenile's behavior in school and at home before deciding what to do.	7. A judge in adult court considers any information that will prove the adult is a responsible citizen.
8. A juvenile can be placed in a correctional school until the juvenile is 21 years old, regardless of the type of crime committed.	8. An adult can be sentenced to life in prison. The sentence depends on the type of crime committed.
9. The delinquent record of juveniles is destroyed after two years of noncriminal activity.	9. If convicted, the adult will always have a criminal record.

not punished. The court acts as if it is the child's parent. The court says it wants to protect and help the child. The juvenile court tries to treat and **rehabilitate** delinquent juveniles.

The adult criminal justice system is designed to punish the criminal and protect the community. An adult who is accused of a crime and taken to court is treated differently from a juvenile who is accused of a crime and taken to court.

As more juveniles commit violent crimes, the courts are increasingly concerned about community safety. This is why some juveniles are sent to adult court when they break the law.

YOUR TURN 12-2

JUVENILE OR ADULT?

Based on the chart on page 82, decide if the following are juvenile or adult cases. On a separate piece of paper, write the word *juvenile* or *adult* for each case. Then decide what in the statement tells you the person is a juvenile or an adult.

1. Carmen is picked up by the police for vandalism. The judge lets her go home with her parents until the next hearing.

2. Ray is convicted of murder and sentenced to life in prison.

3. Susan is picked up for skipping school.

4. Murray has no criminal record, even though he went to court and admitted to shoplifting charges.

5. Chantal asked the jury to find her "not guilty."

6. Mabel listens as a social worker says that Mabel obeys her parents, comes home by curfew, and attends school regularly.

7. Boris is arrested and charged with robbery. He later has a trial.

8. Billy is picked up by the police for running away from home.

9. Pedro will always have a criminal record, even though he has only been convicted of a crime once.

10. Phyllis looks around the courtroom and sees a lot of people watching her trial.

YOUR TURN 12-3

A JUVENILE'S STORY

1. Using the following concept map as a sample, on a separate sheet of paper with the word "Juvenile" in the center, write the facts you have learned about juveniles around the word in the center.

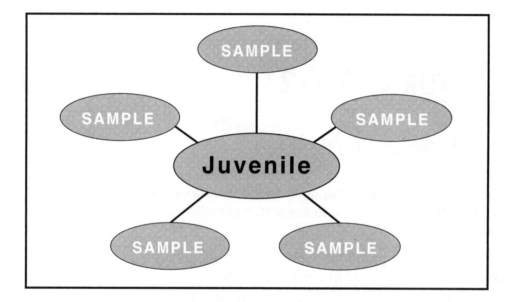

2. Use at least five facts about juveniles to write a story about a juvenile who goes to juvenile court.

LESSON 13

Who Must Attend School

After this lesson you will be able to:

➤ explain the reason for laws which require children to be educated.

➤ tell the difference between private, home, and public school.

➤ identify who must attend school.

WORDS TO KNOW

diploma – an official paper given to a student by a school; it shows that the student has completed the required courses *(noun)*

typical – standard; regular *(adjective)*

guardian – one who has the care of a person or property of another *(noun)*

public school – a free school paid for by taxes and controlled by a government *(noun)*

private school – a school that is set up, controlled, and mostly paid for without government money *(noun)*

home school – a school set up at home by parents who usually serve as teachers *(noun)*

illegally – not done legally; against the law *(adverb)*

truancy – failure of a student to attend school *(noun)*

EDUCATION IS REQUIRED

All children in this country have both a right to a free education and a duty to attend school. In every state but one, there are laws which require children to get an education for a certain length of time. Required education came about because of the belief that educated people make good citizens. Many believe that educated people keep up with what's going on in the country and vote. Most people's chances to get a better job depend on them getting at least a high school **diploma**. For this reason, and many more, public school is free in every state.

Education is usually required from age 5 or 6 until age 16 or 17. Even if you're older than 16 or 17, you have the right to a free public education until you complete high school or until you are 21 years old. You also have the duty to attend school until you are 16 or 17. What does your state require?

Explain the difference between the right and the duty to attend school.

YOUR TURN 13-1

A LAW REQUIRING SCHOOL ATTENDANCE

A **typical** law might read:

School Attendance Requirements

Every parent or **guardian** who lives in this city during the school year and who has custody of a child who has reached the age of 5 years shall place the child in regular attendance in a public or private school or in private instruction. This responsibility of the parent lasts until the child reaches the age of 18 years.

---

1. What does this law say?
2. Why do we have this law?
3. Will everyone understand this law?

PUBLIC, PRIVATE, AND HOME SCHOOL

Parents may choose to educate their children in **public school**, **private school**, or **home school**. Public schools are elementary, junior high, and high schools that are supported by taxes. They are run by local officials. Any child who is between the right ages can attend public school. Public school education is free.

Private schools are not open to or attended by the public. They belong to, and are run by, a particular person or group of people. Schools that are supported and run by religious groups are private schools. It usually costs students money to attend private school.

Some states allow home schooling. Home school refers to parents teaching their children at home. If parents choose home school, they must prove that they can provide their child with a good education that is equal to the education the child would receive at school. Usually this means that the parents must be qualified to teach the child themselves or that the parents must provide the child with a teacher. The amount of time the child spends in home schooling must equal the amount of time the child would have spent studying in school. Whether parents choose private, home, or public school, children are required to get an education.

YOUR TURN 13-2

YOU BE THE JUDGE

Read each of the cases below. Answer these statements about each:

a. Retell the case in your own words.

b. Tell the reasons the child in the case does not attend school.

c. Tell the reasons the child in the case should attend school.

d. If you were a judge, would you require the child to attend school?

Your Turn   **13-2** (continued)

1. Pam is 12 years old. She stays home to baby-sit for her three brothers and sisters who are too young to attend school. Pam's mother works and does not make enough money to pay both a baby-sitter and the bills.

2. Delmas and his parents are from Haiti. Haiti is not in the United States. Delmas and his family came to this country **illegally**. Delmas is 8 years old. He does not attend school because he thinks that the school will report him to the government. If the government finds out that he is here, they'll send Delmas and his family back to Haiti.

3. Elisa is from Spain. She is 10 years old and does not speak English. Elisa doesn't understand the teacher or the other students. She is the only Spanish-speaking person in her school.

4. Karla is blind. She is 5 years old. Karla's parents refuse to send her to school because they think other children will make fun of her.

5. Jerome is 15 years old. He is in the ninth grade, but he hates school. Jerome plans to drop out of school when he is 16. He does not attend regularly now.

6. Isaac is 14 years old. He finished the eighth grade, but refuses to attend high school. Isaac belongs to the Amish religion. The Amish believe in the simple way of life. Most Amish do not use automobiles, telephones, or electricity. They wear simple clothing and live on farms. Isaac's parents believe that if they send Isaac to high school, he will not want to remain Amish. They believe he will want to leave their religion and way of life.

THE JUDGES DECIDE

Judges have ruled on all of the cases above. Read their rulings.
Did you agree or disagree with each judge's ruling?

Case	Decision
Pam	1. You must attend school. It is not your responsibility to provide for the care of your sisters and brothers. The law clearly states that all youth between the ages of 5 and 16 must attend school. Since you are between those ages, you must attend school.
Delmas	2. You must attend school. It does not matter that you are in the country illegally. All schools are required to give a free public education to everyone, regardless of where they came from or how they got here. Schools may not require children to prove they are in this country legally.
Elisa	3. You must attend school, even if you can't speak English. The school's staff members must take steps to provide you with an education. They may teach you in Spanish and English or they may choose another plan, but they cannot ignore you.
Karla	4. You must attend school, even if you are blind. All children must attend school, even if they have a disability. The school's staff members will work with your parents to make sure you are in a school where you can learn. They will decide what school you will attend. The school must provide you with services to help you learn. One kind of service the school may provide is someone to read your books to you. There are also many other services.
Jerome	5. You must attend school until you are 16. You may be detained by the police if you drop out of school before the law says you may. You will be charged with **truancy**. Truancy is failure to attend school.
Isaac	6. You are not required to attend high school. Your right to practice your religion is more important than two more years of required school. The Amish do a good job of preparing children for life in the Amish community.

YOUR TURN 13-3

ATTENDING SCHOOL

Using the following concept map as a sample, on a separate sheet of paper with "Children Who Must Attend School" in the center, write the names of the groups of students who must get an education around the outside.

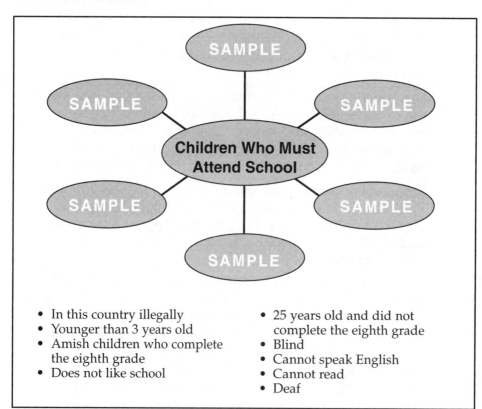

- In this country illegally
- Younger than 3 years old
- Amish children who complete the eighth grade
- Does not like school

- 25 years old and did not complete the eighth grade
- Blind
- Cannot speak English
- Cannot read
- Deaf

LESSON 14

School Rules

After this lesson you will be able to:

➤ read about a school problem and recommend solutions to the problem.

➤ explain what the *Goss versus Lopez* case is about.

➤ state the steps that school officials should follow before suspending a student.

➤ tell the difference between being suspended and being expelled.

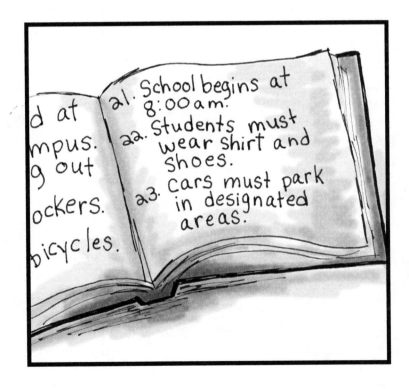

WORDS TO KNOW

school officials – people who work for a school; for example, the
teachers, principal, and security guards *(noun)*

disruptive – upsetting, bothersome, or disturbing *(adjective)*

privilege – an advantage or favor *(noun)*

property – something that is owned *(noun)*

auditorium – a room where a group can gather for a school
assembly or other event *(noun)*

demonstration – a meeting or parade of many people to show
how they feel about something *(noun)*

hearing – an opportunity to be heard *(noun)*

reputation – good name; overall quality as seen by other people
(noun)

informal – not following fixed rules *(adjective)*

Do you have a school handbook? If so, what are some of the rules?

SCHOOLS HAVE RULES

All schools have rules. These rules are mostly made by **school officials** with the help of parents and students. School officials have the responsibility to enforce school rules. There are guidelines for school rules. A school rule must be reasonable and related to students' education. If you fall asleep in class because you were out all night at a party, you may be punished for sleeping in class, but not for partying.

Some states require schools to write the school's rules in a handbook and pass the handbook out at the beginning of the school year. Other states do not. A rule does not have to be written for you to be expected to follow it. What happens if you break the rules?

 YOUR TURN **14-1**

SCHOOLS HAVE RULES

Read the following cases and decide what should happen to the students in these cases.

CASE 1   The librarian asks the school custodian to open all the lockers to look for overdue library books. When she opens Nancy's locker she finds two overdue books and marijuana. She reports it to the principal. Nancy shares the locker with two good friends. She had no idea there was marijuana in the locker. However, she knows that there is a school rule that says, "Do not share your locker." What should the principal do?

CASE 2   Sam is a high school senior. He has been a problem since the first day of class and the teacher is tired of him. Every day the teacher tells him to pay attention and stop disturbing the other students. Sam talks back to the teacher and is **disruptive**. The teacher sends him to the principal's office. Sam needs this class to graduate and says that Mr. Lee, the teacher, just doesn't like him. What should the principal do?

Your Turn **14-1** (continued)

> **CASE 3**   Juan is hanging around the hall to talk to Marilyn. Aaron likes Marilyn also and tells Juan to stop talking to his girl. Juan says he can talk to Marilyn if he wants to. Aaron takes a swing at Juan and they begin to fight. Mr. Lang and Mrs. Brown (teachers) call for help. Mr. Lang takes both boys to the office. The principal talks to Aaron first. What should the principal do?
>
> **CASE 4**   Russell refuses to dress for gym for the third time. His gym teacher has a rule that students who don't dress for gym class go to the office. The teacher sends Russell to the office. Russell tells the principal he doesn't like undressing around other boys and refuses to go back to gym class. What should the principal do?

SUSPENSIONS

Did you recommend suspension in any of the cases you just read? Suspension means that the student is not allowed to attend school for a certain amount of time. Suspension is a common way for school officials to punish students who break school rules.

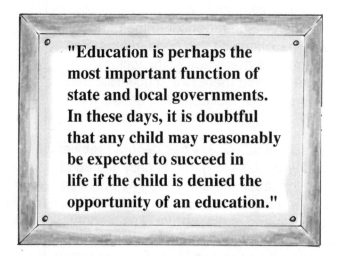

> "Education is perhaps the most important function of state and local governments. In these days, it is doubtful that any child may reasonably be expected to succeed in life if the child is denied the opportunity of an education."

Source: *Quote from the court case of* Brown versus Board of Education.

Until recently, public school officials thought that attending public school was a **privilege** which could be taken away by them. Students who broke the rules were sent home without presenting their side of the story.

Starting with a Supreme Court case in 1954, there was a change in the way people felt about the privilege of attending school. The court said, "Education is perhaps the most important function of state and local governments. In these days, it is doubtful that any child may reasonably be expected to succeed in life if the child is denied the opportunity of an education." Because the Court said this, some people began to believe that education is more than a privilege. It is a right. They believe that if a student is suspended, or not allowed to attend school, the student has a constitutional right taken away. They say the right to an education is taken away. This is true even if the student is suspended for only a few days.

Why would a student want a hearing before being suspended?

Others believe that, while education is important, if a student is suspended for only a few days, the suspension is not long enough to take away the student's right to an education. They also say that it is important to keep order in schools. Suspensions help school officials keep order. What do you think?

Each state has its own laws about suspensions. School officials have the right to suspend or remove students from school in every state. What you can be suspended for depends on what state you live in. Most school officials use suspension only as the last choice. Suspension is typically used when a student does something illegal, dangerous, or disruptive. However, before school officials suspend someone, they are required to follow certain steps. The steps or procedures that a school official must follow came about because of the court case of *Goss versus Lopez*.

 YOUR TURN **14-2**

THE CASE OF *GOSS VERSUS LOPEZ*

Read the case and answer the questions that follow.

 THE CASE OF *GOSS VERSUS LOPEZ*

Dwight Lopez was one of nine students suspended from the Columbus, Ohio, public schools one day in 1971. Some students were suspended because there was a lunchroom fight and school **property** was damaged. Others were suspended because they were among a group of students demonstrating in the school **auditorium** while a class was being held there. Someone else was suspended after she left her junior high school to attend a **demonstration** at a high school. The students all went to different schools. They were all suspended. The principals suspended them by telling them to go home and not come back for ten days. At the end of that time, the students were to bring their parents to school to discuss the students' futures.

An Ohio law gave the principals the right to suspend students without a **hearing** for up to ten days, as long as parents were told about the suspension and given the reason for the suspension within 24 hours. The principals obeyed this law.

The parents went to court. They sued the Superintendent of Schools, Mr. Goss. The parents said that the students had not been treated fairly because they should have been allowed a hearing *before* they were suspended. They did *not* say that their children should not have been suspended.

1. List the reasons the students were suspended.
2. What did the principals do when they suspended each student?
3. Why did the parents go to court?
4. Did the principals break the law?
5. Why might a student want a hearing *before* being suspended?
6. Why might a principal *not* want to have a hearing before suspending a student?
7. If you were the judge, what would you decide?

THE U.S. SUPREME COURT DECIDES

The U.S. Supreme Court decided that students who are suspended for ten days or less have certain rights before their suspension. The court felt that these rights are important to students because a suspension hurts a student's **reputation** and takes away the student's right to attend school. The court said that most of the time suspensions are fair, but suspensions will be even fairer if students are given an **informal** hearing before being suspended.

Students' Rights before Suspension

✔ The right to be told or receive a statement in writing which tells what you did wrong.

✔ The right to be told what the evidence is against you.

✔ If the charges are denied, students have the right to tell their side of the story. This is called a hearing. The hearing can be a simple discussion between a student and a school official.

The Court stated that in emergencies students could be sent home immediately and a hearing could be held at a later date. For example, if a student is fighting, the student can be suspended immediately. The hearing can be held later. The court also said that if a student is suspended for more than ten days, the student must have more protection. For example, if a student is told never to return to school, the student may have an attorney at his or her hearing.

YOUR TURN 14-3

THE DECISION

Answer the following questions about the *Goss versus Lopez* case:

1. Who won the case?
2. What are the three requirements of the Goss case?
3. In an emergency, does the principal have to give the student a chance to present his or her side of the story?

EXPULSION

Students who are expelled are not permitted to attend public school in that school district. Expulsion is a very serious punishment. State laws tell who has the power to expel students. For example, in California only the school board can expel students. Most states do not allow school officials to permanently expel students. However, states do allow school officials to expel students for a certain amount of time. For example, in Connecticut a student can be expelled for 180 school days. That is equal to one year.

Some state laws also list the reasons a student can be expelled. Typical reasons for expelling students are carrying a weapon, causing serious injury to someone, and selling drugs.

◆ **FIGURE 14-1** INTERVIEW FORM

SAMPLE INTERVIEW FORM

Name of Interviewer: _____

Name of principal or assistant principal: _____

Date: _____

School Rules
1. Does your school have written rules?
2. Where can students find a copy of the school rules?
3. What do the rules say about school lockers?
4. What do the rules say about fighting?

Additional Questions:
5. _____
6. _____
7. _____

Suspensions
8. Can students be suspended?   For what reasons?
9. What steps does the school follow to suspend a student in an emergency?
10. What does the school consider an emergency?
11. What steps do you follow if you suspend someone for something that is not an emergency?

Additional Questions:
12. _____
13. _____
14. _____

Expelled
15. Can students be expelled?
16. For what length of time can a person be expelled?

Additional Questions:
17. _____
18. _____

YOUR TURN **14-4**

THE PRESS CONFERENCE

Invite your principal, or assistant principal, to class. Tell your guest that you are studying about school rules and suspensions. Ask questions about school rules, suspensions, and expulsions. Have your questions written before the interview (see Figure 14-1 on page 101). Now write a newspaper article about school rules, suspensions, or expulsions for those who are not in your class.

LESSON 15

School Records

After this lesson you will be able to:

➤ identify three reasons why schools keep records.

➤ list what information belongs in your school record.

➤ tell the procedure for seeing your school records.

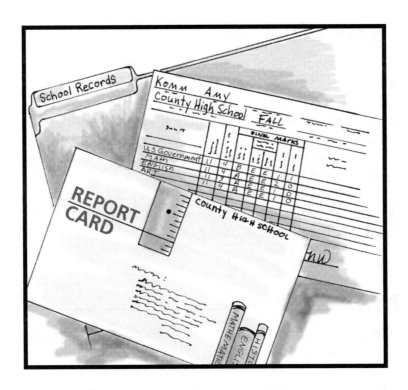

WORDS TO KNOW

records – written evidence *(noun)*

achievement tests – tests you take in school that tell what you know *(noun)*

gossip – chatty talk *(noun)*

misleading – leading in a wrong direction or in a mistaken direction or belief, often by deliberate deceit *(adjective)*

privacy – the condition of being hidden from the view of others; secrecy *(noun)*

exceptions – cases to which rules do not apply *(noun)*

discipline – having to do with orderly conduct or behavior *(adjective)*

WHAT ARE SCHOOL RECORDS?

Have you ever seen your school **records**? School records contain information about you from the time you enter kindergarten until you graduate. Examples are school attendance, grades, scores on **achievement tests**, health records, and notes from your guidance counselor. Many schools keep your school picture in your records.

School records should not have **gossip** or information that is untrue or **misleading**. Remarks such as "speaks strangely to girls" or "has weird political ideas" are not allowed in school records. A parent who believes that his or her child's record contains this type of information may ask the school to change the record.

WHY SCHOOLS KEEP RECORDS

Schools keep records for many reasons. They record your grades to show your progress through school. They keep attendance records to be sure you go to school. Schools keep health and guidance records so that they have information about the whole person, not just that person's grades.

Last Name	First Name	Middle Initial	Grade _____	Home Room _____

_____ Date _____ Adviser _____
Columbia School District   Semester Ending   or Home Room Teacher

SUBJECTS	Subject Grade Level	Semester Period Credits	FINAL MARKS					TEACHER'S SIGNATURES
			Marks in Subjects	Character-Citizenship		Times Absent	Times Tardy	
				Work Habits	Cooper-ation			

EXPLANATION OF MARKS

Subjects
- **A** Superior
- **B** Better than average
- **C** Average
- **D** Barely passing
- **F** Failure

Work Habits and Cooperation
- **E** Excellent
- **S** Satisfactory
- **U** Unsatisfactory

Your signature indicates that you have received this progress report.

_____
Signature of Parent or Guardian
FORM 34-JF 26 B 1999
(STK. NO 44-931822)

Are report cards in your school records?

Schools keep records to send information to others. Some places that request school records are colleges, other schools, the military, the police, social workers, and future employers. Records tell how you did in school. They also tell what special things you did in school, such as making the honor roll.

 YOUR TURN **15-1**

LEA'S SCHOOL RECORDS

Look at the list of information on page 106. Decide if each should be placed in Lea's school records. Give your reasons.

Your Turn   15-1 (continued)

1. Name: Lea May Jones.

2. Address: 2522 N. Capital, Springfield, IL

3. Lea is tall for her age.

4. Lea was born March 14, 1977.

5. Lea's parents are divorced.

6. Lea's kindergarten report card

7. Lea's tenth-grade teacher wrote, "Lea should learn a skill. She is not college material," on Lea's report card.

8. Lea's high school principal wrote a note to the assistant principal. The note said, "I think Lea is a member of a gang."

9. Lea's seventh-grade teacher wrote a note to the guidance counselor. The note said, "Lea acts as if she is gay. Please counsel her."

10. The result of Lea's hearing test

11. Lea belongs to the after-school Bible club.

12. Lea likes to dance.

13. Lea had the measles in the third grade.

14. A note from Lea's ninth-grade teacher to Lea's mother, "Please talk with Lea. She is boy-crazy and spends all day talking to boys instead of doing her schoolwork."

15. Lea's eleventh-grade teacher wrote, "Lea is a hard worker. She will succeed in whatever she tries."

Some employers look at school records before hiring. What information might help them make their decision?

LOOKING AT STUDENT RECORDS

One of the biggest problems concerning school records involves who can see them. Before 1974, some states had laws that allowed future employers, the government, schools, and many others to see a student's records. However, neither the parents nor the student could see the records. As a result of the different laws in the states, the federal government passed a federal law that says, "All parents have the right to see their children's school records." Students who are at least 18 years old or going to college also have the right to see their own records. Additionally, the law says that parents, or the student, must give permission before the school shows the records to others. This law is called the Family Educational Rights and Privacy Act of 1974. Lastly, this law says that if parents find any untrue, misleading, or improper information in the records, they can get it corrected.

The Family Educational Rights and Privacy Act

✔ Students who are at least 18 years old or in college have the right to see their school records.

✔ Parents have the right to see their child's school records.

✔ Parents may see their child's records within 45 days of the request.

✔ Parents may request that any improper information be changed.

✔ A student's records may not be given to any person or agency without a parent's permission. The **exceptions** to this include school officials and others with "educational interest" or to protect the health and safety of the student or others.

 YOUR TURN **15-2**

THE CASE OF THE PROBLEM STUDENT

Read the following case and answer the questions that follow on page 109.

Brian, age 17, is getting ready to apply to college. He asks the guidance counselor for a recommendation from the school. The guidance counselor reviews Brian's school records and finds this note signed by Brian's eighth-grade teacher:

COUNTY CITY SCHOOLS

Columbia Jr. High School ——— ORIGINAL
(School)

COMPLAINT REPORT TO PARENTS

Smith	_Brian_		_202_	_8_
Pupil's Last Name	First Name	Middle	H. R.	Grade

Comments: _Brian has a serious discipline problem. He cannot control himself and will have a problem succeeding in school because of this._

Date _Feb. 2, 1999_   Teacher's Signature _Mrs. Brown_

Mrs. Brown
(grade teacher)

FORM 4J-H65 11RM S-TS 3–72 (S.T.K. NO. 44-754242)

The counselor includes this remark on the college recommendation form.

1. What should Brian do about the comments in his school record?
2. What are Brian's rights under the Family Educational Rights and Privacy Act?
3. What are Brian's parents' rights?
4. Role-play a conversation between Brian and the guidance counselor. Assume the counselor has already mailed the recommendation.

YOUR TURN 15-3

SEEING YOUR RECORDS

Tell where you can get the answers to the following questions. Now answer the questions.

1. Where are student school records kept?
2. How long are student records kept?
3. What is the procedure for seeing my records?
4. How old do I have to be before I can see my records without my parents?
5. Can I give permission for someone to see my school records or do my parents have to give that permission?
6. Who can see my school records without my signed permission or that of my parents?

LESSON 16

Families and the Law

After this lesson you will be able to:

➤ describe some differences between families.
➤ list examples of when law is and is not involved in family life.
➤ give examples of responsibilities that parents have to their children.
➤ give examples of responsibilities that children have to their parents.

WORDS TO KNOW

single-parent – a family with one parent who takes care of the family without the other parent *(adjective)*

abuse – mistreatment *(noun)*

neglect – lack of care; too little attention *(noun)*

custody – the care, supervision, and control of someone *(noun)*

support – to pay the cost of; to provide for *(verb)*

control – to have power over *(verb)*

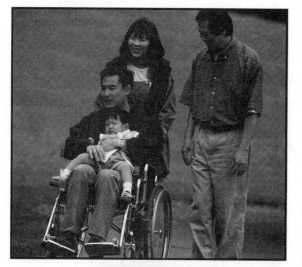

WHAT IS A FAMILY?

What makes a group of people a family? There are many right answers to this question. The family has changed over the years. Not all families look alike. Today the typical family is smaller than it used to be. Couples are having fewer children and, in some cases, no children at all. Some families include a mother, father, and children. Other families include one parent and children. These are **single-parent** families. There are many single-parent families today because:

1. The number of divorces has increased.
2. More unmarried women are having children.

FAMILY LAW

The law affects family life. The law is involved every time there is a birth, death, marriage, or divorce. For example, every state sets the age at which couples can legally marry. The law is involved when you get married, when a child is born, and sometimes when something goes wrong. The law may be involved in cases of **abuse**, **neglect**, **custody**, or divorce.

However, the law usually does not interfere in the everyday life of a family. Most people agree that family life is a private matter. The law usually will not bother you if you argue with your brother or sister or decide to have ten children.

 # YOUR TURN 16-1

THE LAW AND THE FAMILY

Share your ideas about the law and the family. For each sentence, tell if you think the statement should or should not be a law. Discuss your answers.

1. Mothers with young children should not work outside the home.

2. All children should have to go to school until they finish high school.

3. It should be hard for a couple to get married.

4. Wives and husbands should have an equal say about all decisions in a marriage.

5. It should be hard to get a divorce.

6. Adult children should be required to take care of their parents when the parents get old.

7. Beating up one's husband or wife should be a crime.

8. If parents get divorced, the children should be allowed to choose with which parent they want to live.

9. Parents should have to take care of their children.

PARENTS' RESPONSIBILITIES AND RIGHTS

Many families consist of a parent or parents and one or more children. Parents have certain legal duties and responsibilities to their children. According to the law, parents must **support** their children. They must provide their children with food, a home, and clothes. Parents must send their children to school and take them to see a doctor when they are very sick.

What types of clothing must parents provide for their children?

Parents have legal rights, too. Parents have the right to care for their children as they see fit. They may decide where their children live, what they eat, and what clothes they wear. Parents have the right to **control** their children. Parents can require children to work around the house and in the yard. They can require children to work after school. Parents even have the right to keep money that their children earn from a job.

However, parents cannot injure or mistreat their children. If they do, it is called child abuse. As long as parents take care of their children and do not abuse them, the law will not bother parents. They have the right to make their own decisions about their children.

YOUR TURN 16-2

DECISIONS BETWEEN PARENTS AND THEIR CHILDREN

Imagine that you are a parent. Read each sentence. Choose the age group in which you will let your child make these decisions. The age groups are as follows:

a. 1–5 years old   (Preschool)
b. 6–11 years old   (Elementary School)
c. 12–14 years old   (Middle School)
d. 15–18 years old   (High School)
e. 19 years or older   (After High School)

Discuss what age your child will be before she or he makes these decisions.

1. I will let my child decide what foods to eat.

2. I will let my child decide what clothes to wear.

3. I will let my child decide what friends to have.

4. I will let my child decide what TV shows to watch.

5. I will let my child decide what time to go to bed.

6. I will let my child decide whom to date.

7. I will let my child decide how to spend his or her money.

8. I will let my child decide when to drive a car.

9. I will let my child decide to get a job.

10. I will let my child decide to live on his or her own.

Should teens be required to give their paychecks to their parents if the parents tell them to do so?

CHILDREN'S RESPONSIBILITIES AND RIGHTS

The law says that children have certain duties or responsibilities to their parents. Children must follow their parents' rules. This means obeying their parents and going along with parents' decisions. Children do not have to obey parents' orders to commit a crime or to do something which may seriously hurt them. What are some typical rules that children are asked to follow?

The law says that children have rights, too. Children have the right to be supported. Children have the right to food, clothing, and a home. They have the right to education. Children also have the right to medical care, if they are sick. Parents who do not take care of their children may be charged with child abuse.

YOUR TURN 16-3

ADVICE FOR FAMILIES

Read the following cases and role-play them. Advise the family member what to do.

CASE 1 Paul, age 12, is a good baseball player. He is the team's star pitcher. This summer his parents want him to go to Iowa to visit his grandparents. He doesn't want to go. They say he must. He says if he cannot stay home and play baseball, he'll run away. What should Paul do?

CASE 2 Joe is 16. His father died two years ago. Joe's mother doesn't make enough money to support Joe and his younger brother and sister. She asks Joe to go to work and to give his paycheck to her. What should Joe do?

CASE 3 Helga's parents are divorced. She and her two younger sisters live with their father, who works long hours. He does not get home until 8:00 P.M. Helga, who is 16, does all the cooking, cleaning, and child care for the family. Helga wants to go out with her friends after school. She doesn't want to come home and work every night. What should Helga do?

CASE 4 Flora is an adult. Her parents are deaf and in their 70s. They are having trouble paying rent and buying food. They do not want to leave their house for a cheaper apartment, but will have to if Flora doesn't help pay their bills. Flora is just able to pay her own bills. She doesn't know if she can afford to pay her parents' bills too. What should Flora do?

LESSON 17

Getting Married

After this lesson, you will be able to:

➤ explain what the law requires before getting married in your state.
➤ look at a case and decide if a couple can get legally married.
➤ define common-law marriage and explain the laws about it.

WORDS TO KNOW

relationship – attachment between two people *(noun)*

customs – things that have been done for a long time and are widely accepted *(noun)*

forbids – prevents; bans *(verb)*

bigamy – when someone is married to more than one person at the same time *(noun)*

license – a paper, card, or other document showing that someone is permitted by law to do something *(noun)*

certificate – a paper, card, or other document showing that someone has done something *(noun)*

represent – describe; identify *(verb)*

What laws would you require couples to follow before getting married?

MARRIAGE

Out of every 100 Americans, 90 will marry at some time during their lives. Marriage is an agreement between a man and a woman to become husband and wife. It is a personal and private **relationship** which is not generally controlled by laws. However, there are laws that tell who can marry, how to get married, the duties of married people, and how to end a marriage.

 YOUR TURN **17-1**

WHO SHOULD MARRY?

Read these cases and tell if you think the people involved should be allowed to marry. Give reasons for your answers.

1. José is 16 years old. He has been dating Julia for two years. Julia is 15 years old. They want to get married. Should José and Julia be allowed to marry? Give your reason.

2. Aaron was very lonely after his wife died. His oldest daughter, Lori, is a big help with the other kids. Aaron doesn't know what he'll do without Lori. To prevent her from leaving, Aaron decides to marry her. Should Aaron and Lori be allowed to marry? Give your reason.

3. Peter moves to the U.S. from Africa. He wants to follow the **customs** of his land and marry two women. Should Peter be allowed to marry two women? Give your reason.

4. John and Harry have fallen in love and want to get married. Should two men be allowed to marry? Give your reason.

5. Nadia and Anthony plan to marry. Nadia is going to have Anthony's baby. On their wedding day, Anthony changes his mind. Nadia's father gets a gun and goes to Anthony's house to make him get married. Should Anthony be forced to marry Nadia?

GETTING MARRIED AND THE LAW

In the United States, marriage laws are decided by each state. Some marriage laws differ from state to state but all states have requirements.

	Laws about Marriage
AGE	Usually females must be 16 and males 18 before they are allowed to marry. Some states allow younger couples to marry if their parents agree to it. Some states also allow younger couples to marry if they are expecting a baby.
RELATIVES	Every state **forbids** marriage between close relatives. A person cannot marry his or her parent, child, grandparent, grandchild, brother, sister, uncle, aunt, niece, or nephew. Many states forbid someone to marry his or her first cousin.
TWO PEOPLE	Marriage is between two people only. It is against the law to marry someone who is already married. To have more than one husband or wife at the same time is a crime known as **bigamy**.
MAN/WOMAN	States only allow marriage between a man and a woman. Gay marriages are not allowed in any state as of this time. Gay weddings are performed in some communities, but a wedding is only one of the requirements for a legal marriage.
CONSENT	Both persons must agree to the marriage. For example, no one can be forced to marry someone at gunpoint. If a wedding service is forced, it will not be legal.

THE MARRIAGE LICENSE

To get a marriage **license**, a couple must follow some of these steps. Not all states require you to follow every step.

GET A BLOOD TEST A couple must have their blood tested for medical problems that may affect their marriage. A couple can get a blood test at a doctor's office or at the Department of Public Health.

GROOM PERSONAL DATA	1A. NAME OF GROOM—FIRST NAME	1B. MIDDLE NAME		1C. LAST NAME		2. DATE OF BIRTH—MONTH DAY YEAR
	3. AGE (LAST BIRTHDAY) YEARS	4. NUMBER OF THIS MARRIAGE	5A. DATE LAST MARRIAGE ENDED	IF PREVIOUSLY MARRIED 5B. LAST MARRIAGE ENDED BY (SPECIFY DEATH DIVORCE OR ANNULMENT)		6. BIRTHPLACE (STATE OR FOREIGN COUNTRY)
	7A. RESIDENCE OF GROOM—STREET ADDRESS (STREET AND NUMBER RURAL ADDRESS OR LOCATION)			7B. CITY OR TOWN		7C. COUNTY (IF OUTSIDE CALIFORNIA ENTER STATE)
	8A. PRESENT OR LAST OCCUPATION		8B. KIND OF INDUSTRY OR BUSINESS			9. HIGHEST SCHOOL GRADE COMPLETED
	10A. NAME OF FATHER OF GROOM		10B. BIRTHPLACE OF FATHER (STATE OR FOREIGN COUNTRY)	11A. MAIDEN NAME OF MOTHER OF GROOM		11B. BIRTHPLACE OF MOTHER (STATE OR FOREIGN COUNTRY)
BRIDE PERSONAL DATA	12A. NAME OF BRIDE—FIRST NAME	12B. MIDDLE NAME		12C. LAST NAME		13. DATE OF BIRTH—MONTH DAY YEAR
	14. AGE (LAST BIRTHDAY) YEARS	15. NUMBER OF THIS MARRIAGE	16A. DATE LAST MARRIAGE ENDED	IF PREVIOUSLY MARRIED 16B. LAST MARRIAGE ENDED BY (SPECIFY DEATH DIVORCE OR ANNULMENT)		17. BIRTHPLACE (STATE OR FOREIGN COUNTRY)
	18A. RESIDENCE OF BRIDE—STREET ADDRESS STREET AND NUMBER RURAL ADDRESS OR LOCATION			18B. CITY OR TOWN		18C. COUNTY (IF OUTSIDE CALIFORNIA ENTER STATE)
	19A. PRESENT OR LAST OCCUPATION	19B. KIND OF INDUSTRY OR BUSINESS		20. HIGHEST SCHOOL GRADE COMPLETED	21. BIRTH NAME OF BRIDE (IF DIFFERENT THAN 12C)	
	22A. NAME OF FATHER OF BRIDE		22B. BIRTHPLACE OF FATHER (STATE OR FOREIGN COUNTRY)	23A. MAIDEN NAME OF MOTHER OF BRIDE		23B. BIRTHPLACE OF MOTHER (STATE OR FOREIGN COUNTRY)
AFFIDAVIT OF BRIDE AND GROOM	WE, THE BRIDE AND GROOM NAMED IN THIS CERTIFICATE, EACH FOR HIMSELF, STATE THAT THE FOREGOING INFORMATION IS CORRECT TO THE BEST OF OUR KNOWLEDGE AND BELIEF, THAT NO LEGAL OBJECTION TO THE MARRIAGE NOR TO THE ISSUANCE OF A LICENSE TO AUTHORIZE THE SAME IS KNOWN TO US AND HEREBY APPLY FOR LICENSE TO MARRY.					
	24A. BRIDE (SIGNATURE) ▶			24B. GROOM (SIGNATURE) ▶		
	AUTHORIZATION AND LICENSE IS HEREBY GIVEN TO ANY PERSON DULY AUTHORIZED BY THE LAWS OF THE STATE OF CALIFORNIA TO PERFORM A MARRIAGE CEREMONY WITHIN THE STATE OF CALIFORNIA TO SOLEMNIZE THE MARRIAGE OF THE ABOVE NAMED PERSONS. REQUIRED CONSENTS FOR THE ISSUANCE OF THIS LICENSE ARE ON FILE					
	25A. SUBSCRIBED AND SWORN TO BEFORE ME ON	25B. DATE LICENSE ISSUED		25C. LICENSE NUMBER	25D. COUNTY CLERK ▶	
		25E. EXPIRATION DATE		25F. COUNTY OF ISSUE OF LICENSE	BY ▶ DEPUTY	

STATE OF CALIFORNIA DEPARTMENT OF HEALTH SERVICES OFFICE OF THE STATE REGISTRAR OF VITAL STATISTICS   VS 117B (6/81)

Some people believe the fee for a marriage license should be very high. Give possible reasons for this belief.

WAIT BEFORE GETTING THE LICENSE   A couple must wait for awhile after they apply for a marriage license before they can pick it up. After picking up the license, the couple may have an additional waiting period. Each state decides how long a couple must wait. This gives the two people time to change their minds about getting married.

HAVE A WEDDING   A couple must have a wedding service. The law does not require any special kind of wedding service. However, to be legally married, each person must agree to marry in the presence of an official and a witness. Some officials allowed to perform wedding services are priests, ministers, rabbis, judges, and justices of the peace. A wedding service is proof that both people agree to get married. After the service, the couple will receive a marriage **certificate**.

YOUR TURN 17-2

LOCATING RESOURCES

Use the telephone book to locate the office or bureau that issues marriage licenses in your area.

A. Find the section that has government listings. Sometimes this section is blue.

B. Look up "License" under the name of your state. It is either listed separately or under the word "Court."

C. Call the number to get the answer to these questions:

1. How old must a male be to apply for a marriage license in your state? How old must a female be to apply for a marriage license in your state?

2. What is the address and telephone number of the place a person goes to apply for a marriage license?

3. Must a person get a blood test to apply for a marriage license in your state?

4. What does a marriage license cost in your state?

5. After applying for a marriage license, how many days must the couple wait before they can pick it up?

6. Who may conduct a wedding in your state?

COMMON-LAW MARRIAGE

Thirteen states and the District of Columbia allow common-law marriage. Common-law marriage is a marriage without a blood test, a license, or a wedding service. In these states, if a man and woman agree they are married, live together as if married, and **represent** themselves as husband and wife, they have a common-law marriage. Some ways a couple represent themselves as husband and wife are by having a bank account and by filling out income tax forms as a married couple. If partners decide to split up after a common-law marriage, they must get a divorce.

Many people believe that common-law marriage requires seven years of living together. This is not true. There is no seven-year time requirement on common-law marriage. Also, a couple cannot have a common-law marriage if they could not legally marry. For example, as of this time a gay couple cannot have a common-law marriage, even if they live together.

States that do not allow common-law marriage will still recognize the marriage if it took place in one of the states listed below.

States That Allow Common-Law Marriage

Alabama	Ohio
Colorado	Oklahoma
District of Columbia (not a state)	Pennsylvania
Georgia	Rhode Island
Idaho	South Carolina
Kansas	Texas
Montana	

 YOUR TURN 17-3

THE CASE OF THE COMMON-LAW MARRIAGE

Read this case and discuss it with your classmates.

ANA AND EDWARD

Edward Newman and his girlfriend, Ana, live together in Rock Hill, South Carolina. They tell everyone that they are married, but they never bother to get a marriage license or have a wedding service. Edward and Ana buy a house, open a joint bank account, and are known everywhere as Mr. and Mrs. Newman. They are happy until Ana falls out of love with Edward and in love with Rick Roe. Ana leaves Edward and moves in with Rick. Ana and Rick move to North Carolina. Ana still uses the name Ana Newman. After living with Rick for two years, she wants to marry him.

Your Turn   17-3 (continued)

1. Are Edward Newman and Ana Newman married? Give your reasons.
2. What should Ana Newman do?
3. What should Edward Newman do?
4. What should Rick Roe do?
5. Can Ana marry Rick?

 YOUR TURN **17-4**

REVIEWING THE FACTS

Read each statement. Decide if the statement is true or false. If the statement is false, on a separate piece of paper rewrite the statement to make it true.

1. All states require a couple to get jobs before getting married.

2. To get a marriage license in your state, you must get a blood test.

3. A judge can perform a wedding service.

4. Jane and Robert are both 13 years old. They can marry each other in your state.

5. Aaron and Lori are father and daughter. They can marry each other in your state.

6. John and Harry, two men, can marry each other in your state.

7. Elizabeth and Charles live together in Georgia. They tell everyone they are married. They own a house together and have a joint bank account. They are married.

LESSON 18

Teenage Parents

After this lesson you will be able to:

➤ tell whether or not there are legal requirements for teens who want to go to the doctor.

➤ tell whether or not teen fathers may be responsible for paying child support.

➤ explain your school's requirements for pregnant students.

➤ explain how the law proves who are a child's parents.

WORDS TO KNOW

skit – a short play *(noun)*

advice – opinion given as to what to do *(noun)*

narrator – a person who tells what is happening in a story *(noun)*

pregnant – having an unborn child growing within the body *(adjective)*

exceptions – cases to which rules do not apply *(noun)*

emancipated – released from parental care and responsibility *(adjective)*

support – to pay the cost of; provide for *(verb)*

tutor – a teacher who teaches one student at a time *(noun)*

volunteer – to render a service without being required to do so *(verb)*

Patrick and Maggie

Patrick and Maggie is a **skit** about two teens who face a problem. Read the skit aloud in your classroom. When you get to the end of each scene, you'll have a chance to give Patrick and Maggie **advice**.

Players: **Narrator**
Maggie—14 years old
Patrick—15 years old
George—Patrick's friend
Thomas—Patrick's brother

Scene I

Narrator: Maggie, 15 years old, tries to stop her hands from shaking as she calls her boyfriend, Patrick, to tell him the bad news. The phone rings.

Maggie: Hello. May I speak to Patrick?
Hi, Patrick. This is Maggie. I really need to talk to you. We're in trouble.

Patrick: Trouble? What's wrong?

Maggie: I think I'm **pregnant**. This has never happened before. What should we do? I'm scared. I don't have any money to go to a doctor to find out for sure. I don't even know if a doctor will see me without my parents' permission. Do you know? What should we do?

 **YOUR TURN 18-1**

THE CRISIS

Read each question. Discuss your answers with the class.

1. What happened? Retell the scene in your own words.

2. What advice would you give Patrick and Maggie? Why?

3. Can Maggie go to the doctor or clinic without her parents? Why?

4. Who should pay the doctor's bill? a.) Patrick, b.) Maggie, c.) Patrick's parents, or d.) Maggie's parents? Why?

MEDICAL CARE FOR MINORS

Maggie and Patrick are both minors. A minor is a person who is under the age of being an adult, according to the law. Generally a minor must have a parent's consent for medical care and treatment. However, there are a number of **exceptions**. These exceptions are in all states.

A minor must have a parent's consent for medical treatment except:

- in the case of an emergency
- if the law decides that the person is an adult, even though he or she is young enough to be a minor. This is called being **emancipated**. Minors become emancipated when they marry, join the armed forces, or the court declares that they can take care of themselves and make decisions. In some states a female minor is considered emancipated for the purpose of consenting to medical care if she is pregnant or has given birth to a child.
- for special conditions such as addiction to alcohol or pregnancy

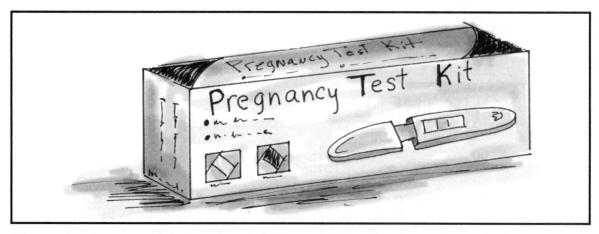

What are the advantages and disadvantages of a home pregnancy test kit?

Scene II

Narrator: The next day, Patrick knocks on Maggie's door. He has a small bag in his hands.

Patrick: Here, Maggie. (He hands her a small bag.) You don't have to go to a doctor. I bought a home pregnancy test kit. Try it. Maybe this whole thing is not true.

Narrator: Maggie takes the bag and slams the door.

YOUR TURN **18-2**

SAY IT ISN'T SO!

Read each question. Discuss your answers with the class.

1. What happened? Retell the scene in your own words.

2. Describe how you think Maggie feels. What questions might
   Maggie ask herself?

3. Describe how you think Patrick feels. What questions might Patrick
   ask himself?

4. What advice would you give Maggie?

5. What advice would you give Patrick?

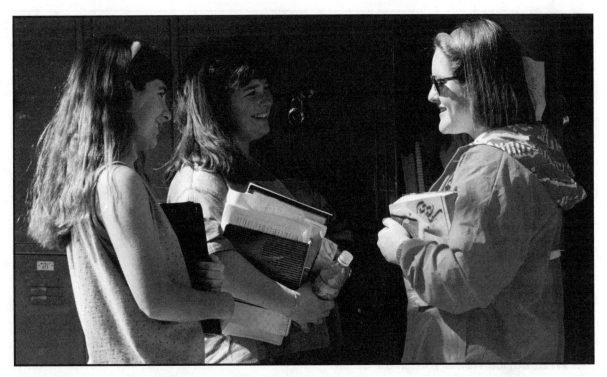

Should a pregnant teen remain in school during her pregnancy?

Scene III

Narrator: One day later, Maggie calls Patrick on the phone.

Maggie: Hello, Patrick? This is Maggie. You won't believe what
                has happened since yesterday. This morning I took the
                test you gave me. I'm pregnant. I was so upset that I
                left the test lying around and my mother found it.
                She's been fussing and crying all day.

                Now she said that I've got to go to the doctor. She said
                that if I'm pregnant, I'm going to have to quit school
                and have the baby. She is going to talk to your parents
                and make sure that you pay for the hospital bills and
                that you **support** the baby.

                Patrick, what should we do? I don't even know if I
                want to have this baby. Can my mother tell me what to
                do? Can she make me have this baby? Can I end my
                pregnancy without her permission?

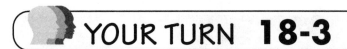

YOUR TURN **18-3**

THE REALITY

Read each question. Discuss your answers with the class.

1. What happened? Retell the scene in your own words.

2. Will Maggie have to quit school?

3. Will Patrick have to pay child support?

4. Can Maggie's parents make Patrick or his parents pay the
   hospital bills?

5. Can Maggie end her pregnancy? Does she need her parents'
   permission?

6. What advice would you give Maggie?

7. What advice would you give Patrick?

SCHOOLS AND PREGNANCY

A pregnant student has the right to continue her education. Many schools give pregnant teenagers the choice of continuing in their school, transferring to another school, or enrolling in a special program during their pregnancy. Some larger school systems offer a home **tutor**. The law requires that the quality of special programs must be equal to that of the regular program.

Although teenage mothers have the right to stay in school after the birth of their children, many do not. Many mothers drop out because they do not have the money or the help that it takes to solve child care and transportation problems.

CHILD SUPPORT FROM A TEEN

Each parent has an equal duty to support a child, regardless of the age of the parent. Usually the parent with whom the child does not live must pay money to the parent with whom the child lives. Most children born to teens live with the mother.

Some fathers **volunteer** to pay child support. However, if a father does not support the child, the mother can go to court. The court may order the father to pay child support. If the father is in school and doesn't work, the court may order the father to pay a small amount of support money. There are cases in which the father is ordered to pay as little as $5 a week. This is done to encourage the father to become a responsible parent. The court then changes the amount of support after the father has finished high school. What do you think of this practice?

Scene IV

Narrator:	After many hours of arguing, crying, and talking, Maggie and her parents decide that Maggie will have the baby. In Maggie's school, she can attend classes until right before the baby is due to be born.
	Since Patrick has no job, he doesn't want to help pay the doctor's bills or child support. As this scene opens, Patrick is discussing his problem with his friend, George.
George:	Patrick, is Maggie going to have your baby?

Patrick:	Yes, and her mother wants me to quit school, get a job, and pay child support.
George:	If I were you, I'd say that the baby is not mine. They can't make you pay then.
Patrick:	Really? If I thought I could get away with it, I might try.
Narrator:	Patrick goes to his older brother, Thomas, who has a daughter. Patrick remembers when Thomas went through the same thing.
Patrick:	Thomas, what would happen if I said that I am not the father of Maggie's baby?
Thomas:	Are you?
Patrick:	Yes, but can she prove it?

 YOUR TURN 18-4

THE DECISION

Discuss your answers with the class.

1. What happened? Retell the scene in your own words.
2. What advice would you give Patrick?
3. Can Maggie prove that Patrick is the father? If so, how?

WHO IS THE FATHER?

Before ordering a man to pay child support, the court must be satisfied that the man is the child's father. Most men admit to being a child's father. If a man denies being a child's father, the mother may go to court. The court may require the man to take a type of blood test called "DNA fingerprinting." Test results from DNA tests are 99 percent accurate.

FILL IN THIS FORM WITH TYPEWRITER OR LEGIBLE PRINTING					

STATE OF ILLINOIS

CERTIFICATE OF LIVE BIRTH

Registration District No.

Registered Number

1. Place of Birth. A. State	B. County	2. Usual Residence of Mother (Where does mother live?)	
		A. State	B. Court
C. ☐ Inside corporate limits and in _____ City, Village, or incorporated Town		C. ☐ Inside corporate limits and in _____ City, Village, or incorporated Town	
D. ☐ Outside corporate limits and in _____ Township, or Road District No.		D. ☐ Outside corporate limits and in _____ Township, or Road District No.	
E. ☐ Name of Hospital or Institution		E. ☐ Residence address (Street and No. or R.F.D. and Post Office)	
F. ☐ If not in hospital or institution, give street & No. or R.F.D. or Post Office		F. Does mother reside on a farm? _____	

3. Child's Name	A. (First)	B. (Middle)	C. (Last)	4. Sex

5A. This Birth was	Single ☐ Twin ☐ Triplet ☐ Quad ☐	5B. If Multiple, Child Born 1st ☐ 2nd ☐ 3rd ☐ 4th ☐	6. Date of Birth (Hour) _____ M, (Month) (Day) (Year)

7. Father's Full Name	A. (First)	B. (Middle)	C. (Last)	8. His Race

9. His Age Years	10. His Birthplace (City and State or Country)	11A. His Usual Occupation	11B. Kind of Business or Industry

12. Mothers's Full Maiden Name	A. (First)	B. (Middle)	C. (Last)	13. Her Race

14. Her Age Years	15. Her Birthplace (City and State or Country)	15. Mother's Mailing Address

17. Informant (Signature)

I hereby certify that this child was born alive on the date noted above	18A. Signature	18B. Attendant at Birth M.D. ☐ D.O. ☐ Midwife ☐ Other (Specify)
	18C. Address	18D. Date Signed
		18E. Illinois License Number

19. Received for filing on	Signed,
	Legal Registrar

A birth certificate is a legal document which is required for every newborn. What information is on the birth certificate?

Scene V

Narrator: Patrick decides to be honest and say that he's the father. Besides, he doesn't want to go to court. He heard that sometimes the judge will make you pay child support even if you don't have a job. Then if you don't pay, you can be put in jail. As this scene opens, Patrick is visiting Maggie in the hospital. She has just given birth to a girl.

Patrick: How was it?

Maggie: Painful.

Patrick:	Maggie, I've decided to help any way I can. I'll pay support in the summers until I get out of school. Then, when I get a steady job, I can help more.
Maggie:	Thanks, Patrick. I sure hope you'll spend some time with the baby too. I'd like for her to get to know you. Guess what her name is?
Patrick:	What?
Maggie:	Her name is Patricia.

The End

 YOUR TURN 18-5

THE RESOLUTION

Read each question. Discuss your answers with the class.

1. What happened? Retell the scene in your own words.

2. Do you think Patrick's child support offer is acceptable? Why?

3. Can Maggie give Patricia, the baby, Patrick's last name?

4. What advice would you give Maggie about the rest of her life?

5. What advice would you give Patrick about the rest of his life?

NAMING A BABY

The mother can give a child any first and last name she desires. The mother can even give the child the father's last name. The father has no legal right to participate in the naming of his child when the parents are not married.

LESSON 19

Divorce

After this lesson, you will be able to:

➤ explain the difference between a separation and a divorce.
➤ tell what a judge needs to know before deciding who gets custody of a child in a divorce case.
➤ define child support and tell why it is needed.

WORDS TO KNOW

marriage counselor – one who gives advice about marriage *(noun)*

separate – to live apart or go in different directions *(verb)*

incompatible – not capable of getting along well together *(adjective)*

unfaithfulness – breaking a promise or vow; being untrue to a person *(noun)*

custody – the care, supervision, and control of someone *(noun)*

SOME COUPLES DISAGREE

Although many couples are happily married, problems occur in all marriages. Minor disagreements are usually solved by the couple working together. Major differences may require the couple to ask a **marriage counselor**, relative, rabbi, or minister for help. Sometimes a husband and wife may think about ending their marriage.

SEPARATION

When marriages break up, the couple may **separate**. If a couple decides to separate, they live apart. The couple is still legally married. They still have responsibilities to each other and to their children. They may get back together at any time or remain separated. If the couple remains separated, neither may get married again. What responsibilities does a couple have to their children, even if they are separated?

DIVORCE

If a couple decides to end their marriage, they may get a divorce. One out of every two married couples gets divorced. Divorce is a big step that will change the couple and their children for the rest of their lives. A divorce is the legal ending of a marriage.

To get a divorce, a court must legally end the marriage. The couple must go to court. Often the husband and wife both have lawyers. After a divorce, legally each person is free to marry again.

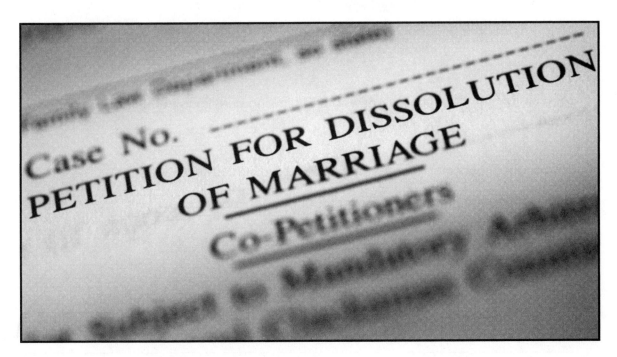

How long does it take to get a divorce in your state?

YOUR TURN 19-1

REASONS COUPLES DIVORCE

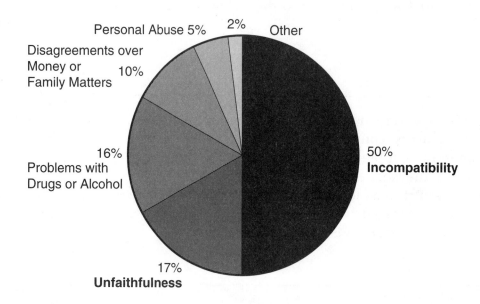

Look at the pie chart above. Answer the following questions about the chart.

1. What is the most common reason couples get divorced?

2. Do more couples get divorced because of physical abuse or because of problems with drugs and alcohol?

3. What percentage of couples gets divorced because of unfaithfulness?

4. What percentage of couples gets divorced because of disagreements about money or family matters?

CUSTODY

If a couple with children separates or divorces, the couple must decide with whom the children will live. In most cases the parents agree. However, if the parents cannot agree, the court must decide. In legal words, the court will decide who will have **custody** of the children.

When a judge is trying to decide who gets custody, the judge may want to answer these questions.

1. How old are the children?
2. Are the children males or females?
3. Do the parents work?
4. How much money does each parent make?
5. What kind of home can each parent provide?

Deciding custody is important. The parent with custody can decide where the children will live and go to school. The parent without custody can usually visit the children at certain times and places. The children can also visit that parent.

 **YOUR TURN 19-2**

WHO SHOULD HAVE CUSTODY?

Read the cases below and role-play them.

1. Wilma and Robert are getting a divorce. They have a four-year-old child. They both work. Robert makes more money than Wilma.

   a. Role-play a meeting between Wilma and Robert as they try to agree on who will get custody.

2. Kareem and Monica are getting a divorce. They have 12-year-old twins, one boy and one girl. Both parents want custody of the children. Both parents work. Monica makes more money than Kareem. They tried talking, but they cannot agree who should have custody. They go to court.

Your Turn **19-2** (continued)

   a. Role-play the meeting between the judge, Kareem, and Monica. What questions would the judge ask before deciding who will have custody?

3. What are the differences between the meeting with the couple alone and the meeting with the couple and the judge?

CHILD SUPPORT

If a divorced couple has children, both people have a duty to provide the amount of money necessary to raise the children. This is called child support. Child support pays for a child's food, clothes, home, and other needs. A divorced couple may agree on the amount of child support needed. If the couple cannot agree, a judge will decide.

When a judge is trying to decide how much child support a parent should pay, the judge may want these questions answered:

1. How much money does each parent earn?
2. How much money does it take to meet the child's needs?

 YOUR TURN 19-3

REVIEWING THE FACTS

Write all of the facts you've learned about the following topics. Make sure your statements are facts, not opinions.

1. Separation
2. Divorce
3. Custody
4. Child Support

LESSON 20

Work Wanted

After this lesson you will be able to:

➤ give examples of when law is involved in the workplace.

➤ give examples of some child labor laws.

➤ name the steps in getting a job and where to find a job opening.

➤ identify examples of unfair discrimination in a help-wanted ad.

➤ identify unlawful questions on a job application or in an interview.

 **WORDS TO KNOW**

discrimination – unfair outlook, action, or treatment based on class or category *(noun)*

qualify – to be fit for some particular work *(verb)*

employer – a person or company that provides a job that pays money *(noun)*

qualifications – any skills, experience, or special training that make a person fit for a particular job *(noun)*

advertise – to call public attention to *(verb)*

employment agencies – places whose business is to find jobs for people seeking them *(noun)*

classified – put into groups according to some system *(adjective)*

application – a request *(noun)*

innocent – blameless; free from guilt *(adjective)*

 YOUR TURN 20-1

SHOULD THERE BE A LAW?

Decide whether there should be a law which protects the workers in each case. Give your reasons.

1. Judy applies for a job as a concrete pourer at a construction company. The job does not require past experience pouring concrete. The owner of the company will not hire Judy because he thinks that the job is too hard for a woman.

2. Lionel is an African American salesperson in a store located in a white neighborhood. He begins to wear his hair in dreadlocks. His boss says Lionel will hurt business if he wears his hair that way. The boss asks Lionel to change his hairstyle. Lionel refuses. The boss fires Lionel.

3. Taylor misses some expensive jewelry from her store. She asks the police to come to the store and search the purses of the three saleswomen who work for her.

4. Maria is 12 years old. She baby-sits for four children during the summer while their parents work.

5. Warren is late for work two or three times a week. He is fired.

6. Howard works in an office with 20 other workers. He smokes cigarettes while in the office. Howard says that he must smoke because smoking keeps him calm. Workers in the office complain about the smoke. They say it is unhealthy.

7. Martha applies for a job as a teacher. She is eight months pregnant. Even though she is the most qualified person, the school does not hire Martha. They need someone to teach for the entire year.

8. Carla is a 17-year-old fast-food cook. She is paid $6 an hour. Last week the company hired Sam as a fast-food cook. He performs the same jobs as Carla. Sam is 47 years old and has three children. The company pays him $6.75 an hour. It says that he makes more because he has a family to support.

LAWS ABOUT THE WORKPLACE

The law affects just about every part of work. There is no single law of the workplace, but there are state and federal laws about workers and bosses. There are laws about safety on the job and equal pay for women who perform the same job as men. There are laws about hiring and laws about firing. Many laws about the workplace are laws against **discrimination**. Discrimination is unfair treatment.

It is unlawful to fire or to refuse to hire a person because of their

- race
- country of birth
- religion
- disability
- color
- sex
- pregnancy
- age

Does your state require young people to get a work permit from school officials?

Discrimination laws about the workplace only protect those who **qualify** for the job. This means that an **employer** can refuse to hire you as a typist if you are deaf and cannot type. However, the employer cannot refuse to hire you as a typist if you can type and the reason for not hiring you is because you are deaf.

CHILD LABOR LAWS

There are laws that control work for young people. These laws are called child labor laws. Child labor laws limit the type of work available to workers under the age of 18. They do not allow young people under the age of 16 to work in factories and limit the hours a young person can work at night. For example, a 14-year-old may work only between the hours of 7 A.M. and 7 P.M. He or she must work no more than three hours a day when school is in session. A 14-year-old must work no more than eight hours a day or 40 hours a week when school is not in session.

Child labor laws do not control all jobs. For example, young people of any age may engage in farm work outside school hours. Can you think of other jobs that young people of all ages may be allowed to perform?

JOB HUNTING

Finding a job is not always easy. You must first find a job opening and then apply for the job. Even if you have the education, skills, and **qualifications** for the job, that doesn't mean that you will get it. Several people may be right for the job. The interview may be what gets you the job (see Figure 20-1 below).

◆ **FIGURE 20-1** GETTING THE JOB YOU WANT

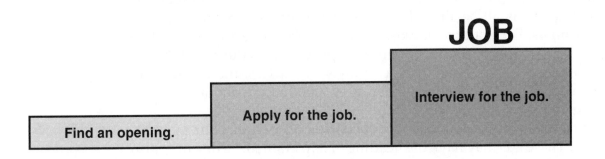

Job openings are discovered in a variety of ways. Sometimes companies tell their workers about the opening. They ask their own workers if they want the available job or know someone who is qualified. It is important to tell friends and relatives that you are job hunting. They may know of an opening. Sometimes companies **advertise** job openings. They place ads in local newspapers, tell school counselors, tell **employment agencies**, post flyers, and put signs in their windows. Look for job openings in all of these places.

To Find a Job Opening

✔ Visit places in your neighborhood. Ask if they have a job opening.

✔ Ask friends and relatives if they know of anyone who is hiring workers.

✔ Ask school counselors if they know of anyone who is hiring.

✔ Read the want ads in your local newspapers.

✔ Look for ads on bulletin boards in your neighborhood stores.

✔ Go to the state employment agency.

HELP-WANTED ADS

According to the law, employers must not discriminate when they seek a worker to fill a job opening. An employer should attract capable workers regardless of the worker's race, age, religion, or sex. If an employer only hires friends and relatives of workers, the workers may all be alike. Therefore, many employers advertise job openings. For example, if workers are mainly white and have white friends, it is likely that most of the people who find out about the job opening will be white. If the employer advertises, the chances are greater that more people of other races will find out about the opening and apply for the job.

Job ads can be found in the **classified** ad part of your newspaper. These ads may have the heading "Help Wanted." They may also appear under headings such as "Employment" or "Employment Opportunity." There are usually a lot of different job openings listed in this part of the paper. These ads tell you the types of jobs that are open. Many job ads tell you how much education you need and if experience is necessary to get a certain job.

According to the law, a job ad should not say that the employer prefers someone of a particular race, age, or sex. This is discrimination. For example, it is illegal for an employer who wants to hire someone to lift heavy boxes in a stockroom to advertise for a "stockboy." The ad suggests that women or older people need not apply. If taken to court, the employer would have to explain why the advertisement was worded like that. If the employer thought that only young males could lift boxes, the employer was probably wrong. There are many females and older people who can lift heavy items.

YOUR TURN **20-2**

IS IT DISCRIMINATION?

Read the following help-wanted ads. Decide if they unfairly discriminate against anyone. If the advertisement unfairly discriminates, rewrite it correctly on a separate piece of paper.

1. Order taker—Make $200–$1,000 a week guaranteed. Now hiring full-time. If you are out of work, an ex-offender, handicapped, under a doctor's care, or homeless call (704) 234-5600.

2. Secretary—Rockville office needs part-time secretary. Looking for dependable, organized person. Experienced in word processing. Send application and photo to 1333 Washington Street.

3. Newspaper carrier—Work as an adult carrier for the *New York Post.* Must have a dependable car and a good driving record. Early morning hours. Apply by calling (202) 123-5544.

THE JOB APPLICATION AND INTERVIEW

An employer uses a job **application** and an interview to decide who to hire. Nearly every job requires some kind of written application. After reviewing the applications, an employer usually selects the most qualified people to interview.

Most job applications have questions for you to answer. They ask who you are and what your education is. They ask what skills and what past job experience you have. The employer asks you to complete the application. It is important to be honest. If you have problems with the application because of a disability, tell the employer you have a disability. The employer must help you, according to the law. If you have a disability and cannot write, you may ask someone to write the application for you. You must tell the writer what to say. If you have a disability and cannot read the application, you may ask someone to read it to you, but you must fill in the answers. The employer cannot refuse to hire you because of your disability. You must, however, be qualified for the job.

A job interview is a meeting between you and the employer. The employer wants to get to know you and will ask you questions. Talk about yourself. Tell about your skills. What else should you talk about? The employer will tell you about the job and the job requirements. Ask questions about the job.

Some Unlawful or Unfair Interview Questions

Arrests	Have you ever been arrested?
Disability	Do you have a disability?
Family	Are you married?
	Do you plan to have children?
	Where does your husband work?
Name	What kind of name is that? Is it Polish?
Pregnancy	Are you pregnant?
Race	What race are you?
Religion	Where do you go to church?
Living Arrangements	Tell me about everyone who lives in your house.

There are some questions employers cannot ask you on an application or in an interview because they are unfair and unlawful. All interview questions should be about your qualifications for the job. If an employer asks you an unlawful question, there are several things you can do. You can (1) politely ask why the question is important, (2) politely refuse to answer the question, (3) answer the question, or (4) try to provide the employer with the information without really answering the question. For example, an employer may ask you if you have ever been arrested. This is an unlawful question because many **innocent** people have been mistakenly arrested. The employer probably just wants to know if you are honest. You can say, "You're probably wondering if I am honest. I have never been in any serious trouble and I am very honest. You may check with my teachers and my past employers." What would you say if an interviewer asked you an unlawful question?

YOUR TURN 20-3

INTERVIEW QUESTIONS

Read each case. Decide if the interview questions asked are fair or unfair. Give your reasons.

Interview 1   Jill Johnson—Assistant Hotel Manager

Jill Johnson is 21 years old. She applies for a job as an assistant hotel manager. Mr. Macki is manager of the hotel. Mr. Macki interviews Jill for the job.

1. Why do you want this job?

2. Do you have experience working in a hotel?

3. Do you plan to get married and have children?

4. Do you have a disability?

5. Will you have dinner with me tonight so we can discuss your job?

Your Turn 20-3 (continued)

Interview 2   Ali Mohabe—Taxi Driver

Ali Mohabe is 25 years old. He applies for a job as a taxi driver. Ms. Baroni owns the taxi company. She interviews Ali.

1. How old are you?

2. Do you have a driver's license?

3. Have you ever had a car accident?

4. Where were you born?

5. Do you pay your bills on time?

A. Write at least five more questions an employer should ask for each case. Make sure your questions are lawful.

B. Role-play each case. Ask all ten questions. Have one person act as the interviewer and another act as the person applying for the job.

LESSON 21

Job Testing

After this lesson you will be able to:
- ➤ identify several types of job tests.
- ➤ match the type of job with the type of job test which should be given.
- ➤ tell different ways to take a test.

WORDS TO KNOW

skills – things you do that come from training and practice *(noun)*

lie detector – a machine that tests if you are telling the truth when you answer questions; also called a polygraph *(noun)*

tester – person giving a test *(noun)*

aptitude – a natural ability; talent *(noun)*

personality – having to do with all the qualities of behavior that make a person different from other people *(adjective)*

attitude – a way of acting or behaving that shows what one is feeling or thinking *(adjective)*

security – related to freedom from danger, fear, or doubt *(adjective)*

urine – a liquid waste product of the body *(noun)*

audiotape – a narrow tape used to record sound that can be played back *(noun)*

promotion – an advance in rank, level, or position *(noun)*

JOB TESTING

Many employers require you to take a test before you get the job. Everyone applying for the job must take the same test. The reason for these tests is to make sure you have the **skills** and the ability to perform the job. There are many kinds of job tests. If you want to be a cashier, the employer may ask you to take a math test. If you want to be a computer operator, the employer may ask you to take a computer test. A job test must relate to the job. For example, if you want to be a cashier, the test cannot be lifting boxes. What are some other kinds of tests employers require?

Why might an employer require a secretary to pass a typing test?

 ## YOUR TURN **21-1**

JOB TEST CHART

On a separate piece of paper, make a job test chart like the one on page 156. For each job, fill in the last two columns with an example of a job that may use the test, and a reason why the test would be used.

Your Turn **21-1** (continued)

Name of test	Describe the test	Job test example	Why use the test?
1. typing	You are asked to type something as fast as you can without making mistakes.	*secretary*	*to find out if you can type and your typing speed*
2. **lie detector**	The **tester** attaches small wires to your arm which come from a machine. Then the tester asks you questions.		
3. math	This is usually a written test with math problems on it.		
4. drug	The tester may take a sample of your blood or ask you for a urine sample.		
5. driving	The tester sits next to you in a car, truck, or other vehicle while you drive. The tester tells you what tasks to perform.		
6. mechanic	This may be a written test. There are questions about how to repair something on it.		
7. medical exam	A doctor will examine you. The doctor may check your ears, eyes, and heart.		
8. **aptitude**	This is a written test with questions that test your ability to learn.		
9. machine operator	You are asked to turn on a certain piece of equipment and make it work; for example, a copy machine.		

LIE DETECTOR, DRUG, AND APTITUDE TESTS

The law is not clear about when and if an employer can use aptitude, **personality**, or **attitude** tests. These tests are usually written tests which contain questions about many different things. These tests tell how you think and feel about things. Some people say employers have a right to know everything they can before hiring workers. Others say that the results of aptitude, personality, and attitude tests are not always correct because some people of color do not score as well as other people, but they think and learn as well as others. For this reason, the law only allows these tests if the employer can prove that the results are correct. The employer must also show that the tests are related to whether the worker can do the job.

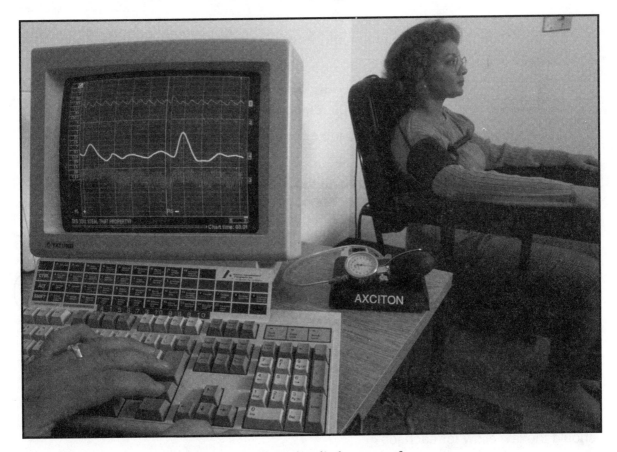

Why can an employer require a security guard to take a lie detector test?

Many employers say that lie detector tests are necessary to prove that the person they want to hire is honest. During the test, the employer asks questions about the information on the job application and whether it was truthful. Employers say lie detector tests help them hire honest people. However, lie detector test results are not always correct. Sometimes, a person can tell the truth and the test will say he or she is telling a lie. For this and other reasons, many states do not allow most employers to use lie detector tests. Some states allow employers to use lie detector tests, but limit the questions they can ask. Laws about lie detectors do not cover people who work for federal, state, or local governments. They do not cover people who work in **security** jobs, either. People who work in security jobs can be required to take lie detector tests.

Some Facts about Drug Testing

1. Many state laws control when and how an employer may conduct drug testing.
2. If an employer requires a drug test, the employer must keep the results a secret and treat everyone equally. This is a federal law.
3. The employer must give every job applicant a drug test, not only those who they think use drugs.
4. The federal government uses drug testing for military, law enforcement, and certain other jobs.

 YOUR TURN **21-2**

WHO SHOULD TAKE A TEST?

In each case, Kareem decides to apply for a job. If you were the employer for each job, which test would you ask Kareem to take? If you were Kareem, would you agree to take the test? Which tests should the law allow for each job?

TESTS

a. lie detector test

b. drug test

c. aptitude test

d. none of the tests

JOBS

1. Cashier in a grocery store

2. Police officer

3. Construction worker

4. Secretary for the county government

5. Dentist

6. Professional football player

7. Airline pilot

8. Ambulance driver

9. Soldier in the army

10. Teacher in a high school

11. Family doctor

12. Taxi driver

13. Firefighter

14. Cook in a fast-food restaurant

WAYS TO TAKE JOB TESTS

There are many ways to take a test. You can answer questions in writing or by filling in answer blanks. You might perform a task, such as changing a tire, or going to a doctor for a health examination. You may even be asked to give a sample of your **urine**.

Sometimes people with disabilities need to take a job test a different way. For example, if you are blind and must take a written test, you can ask someone to read the test to you. You can also ask for an **audiotape** of the test questions. You would take the test by listening to the questions rather than reading them. You could either say the answers for someone else to write or say the answers into a tape recorder. Another example is that people with a reading or learning disability can ask for more time to take a test.

According to the law, people with a disability who apply for a job and must take a test have the right to ask the employer to change the way the test is given. They must ask for the change *before* they take the test. Also, they must tell the employer that they need the change because of their disability. This law is called the Americans with Disabilities Act.

Name some changes people with disabilities might need to have made before taking a job test.

TESTS ON THE JOB

An employer can require you to take certain tests, even after you have been employed. You can be asked to take a test before a **promotion**. This is to see if you are qualified for the promotion. You can even be asked to take a lie detector or drug test while on the job. For example, Patricia works in a store. Her supervisor asks Patricia to take a lie detector test to see if she knows anything about some recent thefts. Whether Patricia has to take the test or not depends on what state she lives in. In some states with lie detector laws, Patricia can refuse to take the test. She is protected from losing her job. In other states, Patricia can be fired if she refuses to take the lie detector test. How can you find out what the law is in your state?

While on the job, you can be required to take a drug test, too. The drug test is for the safety of those with whom you work or the public. For example, a bus driver can be required to take drug tests to protect those who ride on the driver's bus and other drivers. If safety is not a problem, an employer can require drug tests for workers on the job if:

1. the employer suspects people of using drugs.
2. the employer tells all workers that they may be tested for drugs.
3. the employer keeps all results a secret.
4. the employer treats all workers equally.

This does not mean that the employer must test everyone. It means that an employer cannot test you just because you are a certain race, color, sex, religion, or were born in another country.

YOUR TURN 21-3

JOB TESTING

Read each case and answer the questions which follow on a separate piece of paper.

1. Taylor is a very good baseball pitcher and wants to try out for a professional baseball team. He shows up for the tryouts ready to be tested. Taylor is deaf.

Your Turn **21-3** (continued)

    a. What kind of test should Taylor have to take?

    b. Will Taylor need to take any test a different way? If so, what changes should Taylor ask for in the way he is tested?

2. Elaine is an emergency medical specialist. She applies for a job as an ambulance attendant. Elaine has a learning disability. She took special classes at school to help her read. Elaine can read; it just takes her a little longer than it takes others to do so.

    a. What kind of test should Elaine have to take?

    b. Will Elaine need to take any test a different way? If so, what changes should Elaine ask for in the way she is tested?

3. Elizabeth is a security guard at the airport. She has worked there for ten years. She works by the metal detector. Her main duty is to inspect passengers' belongings and prevent passengers from carrying anything illegal on the plane. She especially looks for bombs and illegal drugs.

    a. Can Elizabeth be required to take regular lie detector tests to find out if she has stolen anything? Give your reasons.

    b. Can Elizabeth be required to take regular drug tests to find out if she uses illegal drugs? Give your reasons.

Losing Your Job

After this lesson you will be able to:

➤ identify the differences between a worker being fired, laid off, disabled, or quitting.

➤ identify legal and illegal job loss.

➤ tell about unemployment insurance.

➤ tell about Workers' Compensation.

➤ tell about Social Security Disability.

WORDS TO KNOW

laid off – put out of work, especially for a short time *(verb)*

disabled – unable to move, act, or work in a normal way *(adjective)*

civil service – having to do with working for the government *(adjective)*

employment contract – an agreement on the conditions of employment *(noun)*

union – a group of workers who came together to promote and protect their interests *(noun)*

benefits – advantages; things that are good or helpful *(noun)*

unemployment insurance – an agreement the government made that provides money to employees who are not at fault for losing their jobs *(noun)*

payroll – having to do with a list of employees who are to be paid *(adjective)*

Worker's Compensation – a government program that provides money to employees who are unable to work because of being hurt while on the job, regardless of fault *(noun)*

Social Security Disability – a government program that provides money to people who are disabled and unable to work *(noun)*

LOSING YOUR JOB

You can lose your job for many reasons. You can be **laid off**, **fired**, **disabled**, or you can quit. Losing your job can be very serious. Jobs can help people provide their families and themselves with food, clothes, and a place to live. The law protects some workers against losing their jobs. It even protects some workers who have already lost their jobs.

Job Loss Definitions	
Laid off	When workers lose their jobs because there was not enough work or because the company doesn't have enough money. A layoff may be for a short time or it may totally end the job.
Fired	When workers lose their jobs because the employer dismissed them. Many times the employer decides that the worker is unfit for the job.
Disabled	When workers lose their jobs because the workers' health stops them from doing their jobs or other work.
Quit	When workers end their jobs of their own accord.

KINDS OF WORKERS

Some workers are called at-will workers because they can be hired and fired at the will or wishes of the employer. At-will workers can lose their jobs for any reason or for no reason at all. Also, you can quit a job for any reason or for no reason at all. You do not have to tell your employer ahead of time if you plan to quit. Your employer does not have to tell you ahead of time if you are going to be fired.

People who work for the federal, state, or local government are called **civil service** workers. They are not at-will workers. The government must have a good reason before it hires, promotes, or fires a worker. The reason must be because of what the worker does rather than who the worker is. For example, an employer of a family business can fire an at-will worker in order to hire a relative who will eventually run the company. This may not be fair, but it is not against the law. A civil service worker cannot be fired to make room for a relative. It is against the law.

THE EMPLOYMENT CONTRACT

Some workers have an **employment contract**. The contract is an agreement between the employer and the worker or the worker's **union** (see Figure 22-1 on page 166). In the contract, the worker

◆ **FIGURE 22-1** How a Union Contract Might Look

COLLECTIVE BARGAINING AGREEMENT

for

TEACHERS AND OTHER PROFESSIONAL EMPLOYEES

PART A — STRUCTURE OF THE AGREEMENT

Article 9
FAIR PRACTICES

The Board and the Federation agree that they will not discriminate against any teacher on the basis of race, creed, color, national origin, handicap, sex, age, marital status, or participation or lack of participation in the activities of the Federation.

PART B — BOARD POLICY MATTERS

PART C — PERSONNEL PROCEDURES

PART D — TEACHING CONDITIONS

PART E — SPECIAL PROFESSIONAL CATEGORIES

PART F — SALARY SCHEDULES AND FRINGE BENEFITS

What rules might be contained in a union contract?

agrees to do the job and the employer agrees to pay the worker a certain amount of money. Some employment contracts also cover the reason a worker could be fired and what **benefits** are offered. A contract can be written or just spoken. Since both the worker and the employer agree on it ahead of time, a worker who has a contract can only be fired for one of the reasons agreed on in the contract. Contracts usually say that a worker can only be fired for "just cause." This means a worker can only be fired if there is a good reason. Workers cannot be fired for no reason at all.

The Employee Handbook

Employers often have an employee handbook. This handbook tells what the company's rules are. The handbook contains rules about work hours, dress codes, vacations, sick leave, quitting, and getting fired. In some states, including Arizona, California, Michigan, and Oregon, the law requires an employer to follow the rules in the employee handbook. If the employee handbook says that workers can only be fired for just cause, then the employer can only fire you if there is a good reason. Some employers do not have an employee handbook. Employee handbooks are not required by law.

 **YOUR TURN 22-1**

The Case of Mr. Bistone and Ali

Read this story. Complete the activities that follow.

Ali was a salesperson at a shoe store. His employer was Mr. Bistone. At the time Ali was hired, Mr. Bistone and he talked about the job, the hours, and the pay. Then Ali started the job. No employee handbook exists. Ali liked his job but he often argued with Mr. Bistone. They argued about the shoe displays, Ali's work hours, and other things. All the employees think Mr. Bistone is a strict employer.

One day Mr. Bistone called Ali into his office. He told Ali not to report to work anymore. Mr. Bistone gave no reason. Other

Your Turn   **22-1** (continued)

workers think Ali was fired because he argued with the boss. They think Ali was treated unfairly. Mr. Bistone thinks Ali argued more than he sold shoes.

The workers meet with Mr. Bistone. They talk to him about getting Ali his job back. The workers say that if Mr. Bistone can fire Ali for no reason, he can fire them for no reason. Mr. Bistone does not think he must give a reason for firing a worker in his store.

1. Role-play a meeting between Mr. Bistone and the workers who want to get Ali's job back. If you were Mr. Bistone, what would you do if your workers were not happy about something? If you were a worker, why would you want to help Ali?

2. After the meeting, Mr. Bistone agrees to have an employee hand-book telling the reasons for which a worker can be fired. Make a list of the reasons for which you think a worker should be fired.

If you believe you have been fired illegally, what can be done to try to get your job back?

WHEN FIRING IS AGAINST THE LAW

In the past, most people who worked without a contract had to learn to live with the fact that the boss could fire them for little or no reason, at any time. They had no right to change the boss's actions. Today, although employers can still fire you for no reason, their right to fire is controlled by the courts and by laws. If you believe that you have been fired unfairly, you can go to court and sue to get your job back. This is true even though the law in each state is different.

In every state it is against the law to fire you because of your age (if 40 or older), sex, race, color, religion, disability, or country of birth. In other words, an employer cannot discriminate against a worker. It is against the law to fire you because you are called for jury duty or if you refuse to obey your boss's orders to commit a crime. It is also against the law to fire a woman because she is pregnant or to fire someone who tries to organize a union.

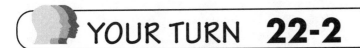

YOUR TURN 22-2

WHEN CAN YOU BE FIRED?

Read each case. Tell if it is legal or illegal to fire the person in each one.

1. Mae-Lee is more than 30 minutes late for work three times each week. Her boss has warned her four times about it. She is still late. Mae-Lee is fired for being late to work.

2. Miguel owns a restaurant. Leona works as the cashier. Miguel asks Leona not to ring each meal in the cash register. He does not want to pay sales tax on each meal. She says no. She is fired.

3. Marsha works as a computer programmer. She is deaf. She requests a sign language interpreter for all staff meetings. Her employer says the interpreter is too expensive. Marsha is fired.

4. Louie has an alcohol problem. He usually gets drunk at lunch. He is warned about drinking on the job. He does not stop. Louie is fired.

Your Turn **22-2** (continued)

5. Winston and Nigel fight at work. Sometimes the fighting damages machinery. Nigel starts a fight with Winston over a car. Nigel is fired. Winston is not fired.

6. Helga works in a bakery. The bakery was recently sold. Helga has a new boss who does not like her. She thinks it is because of her age. Helga is 62 years old. The new boss has made comments about not liking older people. Last weekend Helga was fired. She was given no reason.

Give reasons why a company with more than 100 workers must tell the workers 60 days ahead if it plans to close.

IF YOU ARE LAID OFF

Sometimes workers are not fired but they are laid off. If you are laid off it may be because the company doesn't have enough money to keep you. It may also be because there is not enough work to do. Some layoffs last for a short time. Others last for a long time and end the job. Workers can be laid off, even if their work is satisfactory. When a worker is laid off, the reason for the layoff is not the worker's fault. If your employer tells you not to come back to work, you should find out whether the employer has laid you off or fired you.

All states have **unemployment insurance**. It protects you if you lose your job through no fault of your own. Unemployment insurance provides workers with a small amount of money every week. The amount of money you receive is not as much as you earn while you are working. It allows you to look for another job and still pay some of your expenses.

Money for unemployment insurance comes from **payroll** taxes collected from workers by the federal and state government. The rules about unemployment insurance are not the same in every state. To find out the rules in your state, check with your state employment agency.

Easley,Gina (Larry) 2241 Sterling Dr.	(555) 962-1436	Espinoza, Pedro (Carla) 1344 Broadway	(555) 759-0002
Eckert, John (Lorrain) 780 McLean Rd.	(555) 420-3212	Faber, Jack (Terry) 516 Benjamin Ct.	(555) 620-1050
Eiler, Anita 1849 Dover Dr.	(555) 420-9222	Falkner, Michael (Debbie) 3423 N. Holly	(555) 961-1333
Elwick, James (Susan) 1277 W. Stewart Rd.	(555) 668-6429	Fenton Laura (Robert) 2814 West Shore Dr.	(555) 355-5621
Enberg, Richard (Helen) 1707 Oakes Ave.	(555) 986-6423	Fiedler, Brian (Rosa) 1709 Prairie Lane	(555) 355-1436
Ennis, Rose (Paul) 10630 S. 6th St.	(555) 355-4219	Fisher, Clifford 1419 State St.	(555) 459-3460
Erickson, Don (Helen) 3901 Wilbur Rd.	(555) 910-1312	Flores, Tina (Fred) 2269 Cedarwood Pl.	(555) 420-6234
	(555) 35_____		(555) 625-254_

Where can you find the name of your state employment security agency?

YOUR TURN 22-3

WHO IS AT FAULT?

In each case the worker loses his or her job. Decide if it is the worker's fault or the employer's fault. Should the worker receive unemployment insurance?

1. Mindy is a construction worker. She works outside. Her employer does not call her to come to work if the temperature is lower than 32 degrees. This winter was very cold. Mindy does not work all winter.

2. Anita does not like her boss. She says she will not do any work her boss gives her. Anita loses her job.

3. Lee takes drugs in the men's room. He is caught and loses his job.

4. Harrison stays home a few times to care for his sick children. He has no sick leave left. His boss tells him he is needed at work. Harrison continues to stay home with his children. He loses his job.

5. The company where Sybil works closes one of its offices. She is offered a job at the other office. It is a two-hour drive from her home. Sybil says no to the new job. She does not want to drive so far. Sybil loses her job.

IF YOU BECOME DISABLED

Sometimes workers are unable to work because of their health. This can be for a short time or forever. All states have a law that a worker who is unable to work because of an injury or disease received on the job may get **Workers' Compensation**. This is true even if the worker is at fault. Workers' Compensation is money payments sent to workers or their families to make up for their loss of work. Workers receive part of their regular paycheck. All workers except farm and household workers are covered by this law.

Laws like the Americans with Disabilities Act make it easier for workers with disabilities to have a job. It is illegal to fire someone because of a disability. However, sometimes people have a disability which prevents them from working. Usually the worker and his or her doctor make this decision. States have laws that say if you become disabled and unable to work, then you may receive money payments called **Social Security Disability**.

Social Security Disability is a federal program. The law requires your employer to take money from your paycheck to help pay it. Additionally, the law requires your employer to pay a Social Security tax for each worker. You can only receive Social Security Disability if you and your employer pay Social Security tax.

 YOUR TURN **22-4**

HELP FOR WORKERS WHO LOSE THEIR JOBS

Read each case. In each one, the worker loses his or her job. Tell if the worker should ask for unemployment insurance, Workers' Compensation, or Social Security Disability.

1. Harry was laid off when the company closed the plant he worked in.

2. Laura is a bus driver. She has a disease which causes her to become blind. The company where Laura works has no other job that Laura can do. Laura loses her job.

3. Earlene is a butcher. At work, she cuts off her finger while slicing some meat. Earlene cannot work for three months.

4. Pierre is a coal miner. He gets black lung disease and can no longer work. Black lung disease is caused by dust in coal mines.

5. Sandy is a teacher. She stops working because she has AIDS and is too weak. Her doctor advised her to do so.

IF YOU QUIT

You can quit a job for any reason or for no reason. There are no laws about how to quit a job. However, a worker usually tells her or his employer about leaving a few weeks before it happens. This is called "giving notice." This allows your employer to find another worker.

LESSON 23

Places to Live

After this lesson you will be able to:
- ➤ identify places to live in the community.
- ➤ list things to consider before deciding where to live.
- ➤ define discrimination.
- ➤ discuss discrimination in housing.

175

WORDS TO KNOW

suburb – a place that is near the outskirts of a city *(noun)*

rural – having to do with the country or the people who live there *(adjective)*

appliances – machines made for a particular use in a house or office, like a fan or a refrigerator *(noun)*

income – the amount of money or pay earned or received *(noun)*

vacancy – a place such as an apartment that is not occupied *(noun)*

complaint – an expression of dissatisfaction or pain *(noun)*

PLACES TO LIVE

Every year millions of Americans move from one home to another. There are many things to think about when choosing a place to live. Some families choose to live in a large city while others choose to live in a small town, a **suburb**, or a **rural** area. Some families choose to live in an apartment, while others choose a single-family house, a walk-up flat, or a mobile home. Some families choose to rent while others choose to own a home.

Do you live with other family members? Have you ever thought about buying a house of your own? In recent years, it has become more and more difficult for people to buy houses. That is because the cost of houses has increased. Many people rent the places where they live, especially when they first move away from home.

What things would you consider when looking for a place to live?

Some Things to Consider before Renting

✔ How much is the rent? Can I afford it?

✔ How many rooms do I need? How many bedrooms do I need?

✔ Should the place be furnished?

✔ Are there closets?

✔ Is it clean and in good repair?

✔ What kind of heat does it have? Is the cost of heat included in the rent
payment?

✔ Do I need air conditioning?

✔ Is the place safe? Do the doors and windows have locks?

✔ Do the gas and electricity work?

✔ What major **appliances** come with the house (stove, refrigerator, washing
machine, dryer)? Do I need to buy others?

✔ What services do I need (garbage pick-up, pool, cable TV)? Who pays
for them?

✔ Are pets allowed?

✔ What do I want to be near (friends, ball field, work, school, grocery store)?

✔ Do I need public transportation?

 YOUR TURN **23-1**

CHOOSING A PLACE TO RENT

Read each case and discuss the questions which follow.

1. Pete and Arsenio just finished high school and have new jobs.
   They want to share a place to live. Pete works in a drugstore from
   9:00 A.M. to 5:00 P.M. five days a week. He takes home $575 a
   month and has an old car. Arsenio works from 3:00 P.M. to 11:00
   P.M. five nights a week in a local factory. He takes home $850 a
   month. He does not have a car. Arsenio has a cat.

Your Turn **23-1** (continued)

   a. How much money will Pete and Arsenio together bring home
      each month?

   b. Do you think Arsenio should pay more for rent than Pete since
      he makes more money? Give your reasons.

   c. What special things does Pete need to consider before renting?

   d. What special things does Arsenio need to consider before
      renting?

   e. Role-play the conversation between Pete and Arsenio when
      they discuss their housing needs.

2. Sophia is 20 years old and has dropped out of high school. She
   has a two-year-old child. She could earn $50 a week caring for two
   other children during the day. She also receives a check from Aid
   to Families with Dependent Children (AFDC) of $240 a month
   (AFDC is sometimes called welfare).

   a. How much money will Sophia have each month?

   b. What special things does Sophia need to consider before
      renting?

   c. Advise Sophia what to do concerning renting a place to live.

3. Don and Earlene Johnson both have jobs. Together they earn
   about $3,000 a month. They have three children in elementary
   school and own one car. Don likes to go to the gym to play
   basketball about three times a week. The children have a dog.

   a. What special things do the Johnsons need to consider before
      renting?

   b. Advise them what to do concerning renting a place to live.

WHAT IS AVAILABLE?

   Many people look in the newspaper for a list of available
places to live. You can also call a real estate office to help you.
Some people find apartments or houses by asking friends about
available places.

FOR RENT

2 Bedroom apartment, 1 full bath, large living room, plus dining area. The kitchen is equipped with the latest appliances. The living room contains a built-in entertainment center that's great for family get-togethers and sporting events. Call John to make an appt. to walk-through this fabulous apartment.

You'll love it!   Tel. (555) 221-4321

List ways to find apartments that are for rent.

WHAT IS DISCRIMINATION?

Discrimination is treating one person differently than another person. If you are looking for a house or apartment to rent, you should know the laws about discrimination. A property owner who wants to rent out a house or apartment should also know these laws.

 YOUR TURN **23-2**

THE CASE OF THE UNWANTED TENANT

Read the following story. Discuss it with your class.

Since the death of her husband, Mrs. Amy Weaver has run a five-unit apartment house. She lives in one unit. She makes her **income** by renting the other four. Several of her tenants have threatened to move if she rents to people of color. She does not dislike people of color, but feels she has the right to do whatever she wants with her own building.

Your Turn 23-2 (continued)

> Mr. Van Tran, from Vietnam, is looking for an apartment to rent. A friend at work tells Mr. Van Tran about a **vacancy** at Mrs. Weaver's. Mr. Van Tran calls and makes an appointment to see the apartment. When Mr. Van Tran arrives to look at the apartment, Mrs. Weaver takes one look at him and tells him the apartment has been rented. "After all," she says to herself, "it's my property, and no one has the right to tell me who can live here."

1. List the reasons Mrs. Weaver should not be required to rent to Mr. Van Tran.

2. List the reasons Mrs. Weaver should be required to rent to Mr. Van Tran.

3. Do you think Mr. Van Tran should be allowed to live wherever he wants?

4. Do you think Mrs. Weaver should be allowed to rent to whomever she wishes?

5. Should there be laws which tell property owners to whom they can rent? Give your reasons.

It is illegal to discriminate because of a person's:

- sex
- race
- color of skin
- religion
- family status
- country of birth
- disability

A property owner can choose one renter over another as long as the reason is not illegal. When a person treats or selects one person over another, he or she discriminates. Some discrimination is illegal and some is not. Suppose a family of six wants to rent a two-bedroom apartment or a person with bad credit wants to rent a house. The property owner can legally discriminate against the possible renters. Suppose a person who is Muslim wants to rent a house. The owner cannot refuse to rent to a person if the only reason for refusing is the person's religion.

EQUAL HOUSING OPPORTUNITY

We Do Business in Accordance With the Federal Fair Housing Law

(Title VIII of the Civil Rights Act of 1968, as Amended by the Housing and Community Development Act of 1974)

IT IS ILLEGAL TO DISCRIMINATE AGAINST ANY PERSON BECAUSE OF RACE, COLOR, RELIGION, SEX, OR NATIONAL ORIGIN

- In the sale or rental of housing or residential lots
- In advertising the sale or rental of housing
- In the financing of housing
- In the provision of real estate brokerage services

Blockbusting is also illegal

An aggrieved person may file a complaint of a housing discrimination act with the:

U.S. DEPARTMENT OF HOUSING AND URBAN DEVELOPMENT
Assistant Secretary for Fair Housing and Equal Opportunity
Washington, D.C. 20410

What is the telephone number of the HUD office nearest to you?

If you think you have been discriminated against, you may file a **complaint** with a state or local agency that deals with housing discrimination in the U.S. Department of Housing and Urban Affairs (HUD). These agencies have the power to look into your complaint and either solve the problem or file a lawsuit for you.

 YOUR TURN **23-3**

Is It Discrimination?

Read each case. Answer these questions about each one.

a. Was there discrimination? If so, by whom?

b. If there was discrimination, was it legal or illegal?

Your Turn **23-3** (continued)

1. A woman looking for a two-bedroom apartment is turned down by the owner. The owner thinks the apartment is too small for her and three children.

2. A property owner turns down a man who receives government disability checks as income. The owner is worried that the man won't be able to pay the rent.

3. A property owner refuses to rent a house to a Latino couple. She thinks that the neighbors won't approve.

4. A woman is rejected for an apartment. The owner believes the woman's divorce makes her unable to pay.

5. A group is interested in renting a house for people with AIDS. The owner will not rent it to them.

6. A young man is rejected because he looks like a heavy-metal musician. The owner thinks the man might make too much noise.

7. A young deaf couple wants to rent an apartment. They request that the smoke alarms and doorbell be replaced with ones that flash. The owner thinks the deaf couple is expecting too much and rejects them.

LESSON 24

Landlord Rights and Responsibilities

After this lesson you will be able to:

➤ define landlord and tenant.
➤ list the responsibilities of a landlord.
➤ tell what action a landlord can take if something goes wrong in a house or apartment.

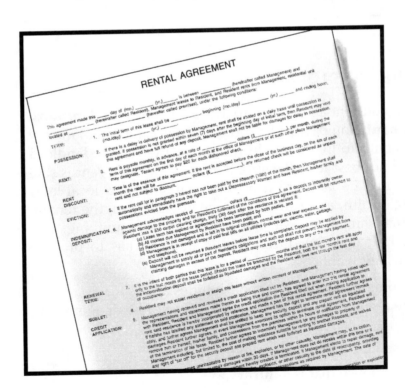

WORDS TO KNOW

landlord – the person who owns a house or apartment and rents it to tenants *(noun)*

tenant – the person renting and living in a house or apartment *(noun)*

sanitary – free from germs and dirt *(adjective)*

lease – a contract between a landlord and tenant for use of property such as an apartment or house *(noun)*

security deposit – payment given to secure rented property; usually the amount is one month's rent—the money is used in case the tenant damages the apartment or moves *(noun)*

cookware – pots and pans *(noun)*

demonstrations – showing how to do something *(noun)*

eviction – putting a tenant out by legal process *(noun)*

WHO IS THE LANDLORD?

The person you rent a house or apartment from is the **landlord**. You are the **tenant**. You pay the landlord a certain amount of money or rent each month to live there. In return for money, the landlord must do his or her best to make sure that the place you rent is safe and fit to live in. The landlord must obey all state and local laws about housing, health, and safety. This means that you, the tenant, can expect such things as heat, hot water, lights, plumbing, and doors that lock. It does not mean that a landlord has to provide everything a tenant wants.

The most common landlord responsibilities are:
- to provide a safe house. The house should not be dangerous to live in.

- to provide a house that is fit to live in.

- to provide a house that is **sanitary**.

- to provide a house that the tenant can enjoy without being disturbed.

What's the difference between a landlord and a tenant?

 ## YOUR TURN **24-1**

RULES FOR LANDLORDS AND TENANTS

1. You are the landlord. Make a list of rules you want tenants to follow while renting your three-bedroom house.

2. You are a tenant. Make a list of rules you want your landlord to follow while you rent her or his three-bedroom house.

3. Role-play the discussion between the landlord and the tenant as they try to reach an agreement concerning each other's rules.

4. Write the agreed-upon rules on one piece of paper. Have the tenant and the landlord sign the paper. This agreement can become part of a **lease**.

◆ **FIGURE 24-1** SAMPLE LEASE

RANDALL REAL ESTATE CO.
PROPERTY MANAGEMENT-INVESTMENT
PROPERTY-SALES-INSURANCE

THIS AGREEMENT, Made and executed this day *3* day of November A.D., 1998 by and between RANDALL REAL ESTATE COMPANY, hereinafter call the Landlord, and _____ *Tina Marie Wilder* _____ , hereinafter called the Tenant.

WITNESSETH, That Landlord does hereby let unto Tenant the premises known as Apartment No. 301, at 12 Marshall Street in Johnstown, for the term commencing on the *1* day of *December*, *1998*, and fully ending at midnight on the day of *November 30,*, *1999*, at and for the total rental of *$685.00* Dollars, the first installment payable on the execution of this agreement and the remaining installments payable in advance on the *1st* day of each ensuing month, to and at the office of RANDALL REAL ESTATE COMPANY, 100 Columbia Road, in Johnstown.

On the *1st* day of *December*, *1998*, a sum of *$685.00* shall become due and payable. This sum shall cover the period up to the day of *January 1st*, *1999*; thereafter, a sum of *$685.00* shall be due and payable on the *1st* day of each month.

AND TENANT does hereby agree as follows:

1. Tenant will pay the rent as specified.
2. Tenant will pay all utility bills as they become due.
3. Tenant will use the premises for a dwelling and for no other purpose.
4. Tenant will not use the premises for any unlawful purpose, or in any noisy and rowdy manner, or in a way offensive to any other occupant of the building.
5. Tenant will not transfer or sublet the premises without the written consent of the landlord.
6. Landlord shall have access to the premises at any time for the purpose of inspection, to make repairs the Landlord considers necessary, or to show the apartment to tenant applicants.
7. Tenant will give Landlord prompt notice of any defects or breakage in the structure, equipment, or fixtures of said premises.
8. Tenant will not make any alterations or additions to the structure, equipment, or fixtures of said premises without the written consent of the Landlord.
9. Tenant will pay a security deposit in the amount of _____ *$150.00* , which will be held by Landlord until expiration of this lease and refunded on the condition that said premises is returned in good condition, normal wear and tear expected.
10. Tenant will not keep any pets, live animals, or birds of any description in said premises.
11. Landlord shall be under no liability to Tenant for any discontinuance of heat, hot water, or elevator service, and shall not be liable for damage to property of Tenant caused by rodents, rain, snow, defective plumbing, or any other source.
12. Should Tenant continue in possession after the end of the term herein with permission of Landlord, it is agreed that the tenancy thus created can be terminated by either party giving to the other party not less than Thirty (30) day's Written Notice.
13. Tenant shall be required to give the Landlord at least thirty (30) days notice, in writing, of his or her intention to vacate the premises at the expiration of his tenancy. If Tenant vacates the premises without first furnishing said notice, Tenant shall be liable to the Landlord for one month's rent.
14. Both landlord and Tenant waive trial by jury in connection with any agreement contained in the rental agreement or any claim for damages arising out of the agreement or connected with this tenancy.
15. Landlord shall not be held liable for any injuries or damages to the Tenant or his or her guests, regardless of cause.
16. In the event of increases in real estate taxes, fuel charges, or sewer and water fees, Tenant agrees during the term of the lease to pay a proportionate share of such charges, fees, or increases.
17. Tenant confesses judgement and waives any and all rights to file a counterclaim, or a defense to any action filed by the Landlord against the Tenant and further agrees to pay attorney's fees and all other costs incurred by the Landlord in an action against the Tenant.
18. Tenant agrees to observe all such rules and regulations which the Landlord or his agents will make concerning the apartment building.

IN TESTIMONY WHEREOF, Landlord and Tenant have signed this Agreement the day and year first hereinbefore written.

Signed in the presence of

_____

_____

Tina Marie Wilder

_____

Tabitha Jones, Resident Manager

THE LEASE

Sometimes the landlord asks the tenant to sign a lease before the tenant moves into an apartment or house (see Figure 24-1). A lease is an agreement between the landlord and tenant which is signed by both parties. It tells the rights and responsibilities of the landlord and the tenant.

What Is in a Lease?

- the address of the property
- the amount of the rent
- the date the rent is due each month
- the time period covered by the lease
- the amount of any **security deposit**
- the conditions under which rent can be raised
- rules about repairs

Read the lease carefully before signing it. If there are parts of the lease with which you don't agree, discuss it with the landlord. If agreement is reached, the tenant and landlord can draw a line through the part of the lease which no longer applies.

 YOUR TURN 24-2

THE LEASE

Read the sample lease and answer these questions:

1. Who is the landlord?

2. Who is the tenant?

3. What is the address of the rental property?

4. How much is the rent and when is it due?

5. How much is the security deposit?

Your Turn **24-2** (continued)

6. Can the tenant have pets?

7. Who is responsible for repairs?

8. Can the landlord go into the tenant's house at any time? Give the reason for your answer.

9. What can the landlord do if the rent is late?

THE SECURITY DEPOSIT

Sometimes a landlord requires you to pay a security deposit before moving into an apartment or house. A security deposit is money paid by the tenant to the landlord. Many landlords require new tenants to pay an amount equal to one or two months' rent. The purpose of a security deposit is to protect the landlord. If you move out early or damage the property, the landlord can pay for the damages with the security deposit. The landlord does not have to go to court to collect the money due.

Landlords are not allowed to use the security deposit to pay for repairs caused by normal wear and tear. Examples of normal wear and tear are if the outside paint begins to peel after seven years, or if the hallway carpet is worn because it has not been replaced in ten years. Tenants and landlords frequently disagree about what wear and tear is normal.

 YOUR TURN 24-3

WHO SHOULD PAY?

Read the cases below. In each one, the tenant is moving out. Decide who should pay for the damages in each case. If the tenant is responsible, the landlord gets to keep some of the tenant's security deposit.

1. The tenant moves out without cleaning the apartment. The landlord must remove the trash, clean the walls and floors, clean the oven and refrigerator, and wash the windows. Who should pay for cleaning the apartment? Give your reasons.

2. The toilet overflows in an upstairs apartment. The water leaks through the floor. It ruins the ceiling and carpet in the apartment below. Who should pay for the new ceiling and carpet in the downstairs apartment? Who should pay to fix the toilet in the upstairs apartment? Give your reasons.

3. The tenant has a pet cat. The cat stains the carpet. The lease allows tenants to have pets. Who should pay for cleaning the carpet? Give your reasons.

4. The walls of the apartment are faded and need to be repainted. Who should pay for the paint job? Give your reasons.

5. The stove in an apartment stops working. The repairperson says it is worn out and should be replaced. The tenant's job is selling **cookware**. The tenant has many cooking **demonstrations** in the apartment. Who should pay for the new stove? Give your reasons.

6. The roof leaks and ruins the hardwood floors. The tenant never told the landlord about the leak. Who should pay to have the floors repaired? Give your reasons.

EVICTING A TENANT

Sometimes tenants don't live up to their responsibilities. They may break the rules in the lease. If this happens, the landlord has certain rights. The landlord and the tenant can talk to try to solve the problem. They may agree to end the lease before the lease period is over. If the problem is serious and there is no agreed-upon solution, the landlord may have the tenant evicted. An **eviction** is a legal action to have the tenant forced off the property.

Some Reasons for Evicting a Tenant

✔ not paying rent
✔ being too noisy all the time
✔ committing a crime on the property
✔ damaging the apartment

What do you think is the most common reason for eviction?

If the landlord wants to evict the tenant, the landlord cannot suddenly throw the tenant out of the apartment. The landlord must file a case in court. In some areas this takes place in regular civil court. In other places there is a special housing court or Tenant-Landlord Commission. The court or commission decides whether the tenant can be evicted. If you receive a court announcement that your landlord intends to evict you, respond immediately. Do not ignore the announcement. Talk to your landlord. Be sure you show up in court, even if you are late paying rent and don't yet have the money. The judge may allow you more time to pay. If you don't go to court, the judge will rule in favor of the landlord without hearing your side.

YOUR TURN 24-4

EDWARDS VERSUS HABIB

Read this case. Decide what you would do in this case.

Mr. Edwards rented a house from Ms. Habib. Shortly after moving in, Mr. Edwards lost his job. He did not pay the rent for two months. Ms. Habib sent several notices to Mr. Edwards that the rent was late. Since Mr. Edwards didn't have any money, he ignored the notices. At the beginning of the third month, Mr. Edwards got a new job, but it was too late. Ms. Habib had already filed a request to have Mr. Edwards evicted. Mr. Edwards has a notice on his door. He receives another notice in the mail. The notice states that Ms. Habib intends to evict Mr. Edwards. It says that there will be a hearing in Tenant-Landlord Court on the tenth of the month. Mr. Edwards likes the house and wants to continue living there.

1. Tell what happened in this case. Only tell the facts.

2. What does Mr. Edwards want? List all of the things Mr. Edwards can do. Discuss the advantages and disadvantages of each of Mr. Edwards's solutions.

3. What does Ms. Habib want? List all of the things Ms. Habib can do. Discuss the advantages and disadvantages of each of Ms. Habib's solutions.

Your Turn   **24-4** (continued)

4. What should Mr. Edwards do?

5. What should Ms. Habib do?

6. Role-play the eviction hearing between the judge, Mr. Edwards, and Ms. Habib.

LESSON 25

Tenant Rights and Responsibilities

After this lesson you will be able to:

➤ name some responsibilities of a tenant when renting a place to live.

➤ decide what to inspect before leasing an apartment.

➤ tell what action a tenant can take if something goes wrong in an apartment.

INTENTION TO VACATE

Date: _____

To: _____

From: _____ the undersigned intends to move from

This notice that on (date) _____ the residence at (address) _____

The undersigned understands that the lease/rental agreement requires _____ days of notice. The days of advance notice, and that this represents _____ days of notice. The undersigned also understands that he/she is responsible for paying rent through the end of the notice period required in the lease/rental agreement or until another tenant approved by the management has moved in, whichever occurs first.

The undersigned understands that any deposits that he/she is entitled to will be refunded within _____ days after the premises have been vacated and all keys returned to the management, so long as the dwelling is left in broom-clean condition and undamaged.

Reasons for leaving: _____

Forwarding address: _____

WORDS TO KNOW

security deposit – payment given to secure rented property; usually the amount is one month's rent—the money is used in case the tenant damages the apartment or moves *(noun)*

utility – having to do with a useful service or product such as water, gas, electricity, or telephone service provided to the public *(adjective)*

appliances – machines made for a particular use in a house or office, like a fan or a refrigerator *(noun)*

accommodation – an adjustment that meets a need *(noun)*

inspect – to look at carefully *(verb)*

rodents – animals that have sharp front teeth for gnawing, such as mice or rats *(noun)*

housing codes – body of laws set down in a clear and orderly way to regulate housing *(noun)*

minimum – the smallest amount or number that is possible *(adjective)*

Can you do anything you want to if you rent an apartment?

IF YOU ARE THE TENANT

One day you may want to get your own apartment. The person you rent the apartment from, the landlord, has certain rights and responsibilities. You, the tenant, have rights and responsibilities too.

Tenant Responsibilities

✔ Pay a **security deposit**, if required.

✔ Pay the rent on time.

✔ Pay all **utility** bills, if they are not covered in the rent.

✔ Use the apartment only for legal activities.

✔ Quickly inform the landlord of any defects or damage to the apartment or **appliances** so the landlord can make repairs.

✔ Keep the apartment clean.

✔ Keep noise to a reasonable level so others are not disturbed.

✔ Stay in the apartment for the whole time of the lease.

✔ Tell the landlord if you need an **accommodation**.

If you have a disability, you must ask the landlord for what you need to live in the apartment. This may include asking the landlord to build a ramp next to the front-door stairs, to put in a flashing smoke alarm in the apartment, or to allow you to put in a flashing doorbell. This is called an accommodation. It is your responsibility to ask for the accommodation. The landlord does not have to guess what you may need.

 YOUR TURN **25-1**

THE CASE OF THE NOISY NEIGHBOR

Read the case and answer the questions which follow.

Your Turn **25-1** (continued)

Judy and Tom Deemer sign a lease and move into an apartment building in their favorite neighborhood. Soon after moving in, they discover that the other tenant is really noisy. During the first week, their next-door neighbor throws several wild parties, keeping the Deemers up all night. When their neighbor isn't throwing parties, he has visitors who come at all hours of the day and night. They constantly slam the doors. The visitors look rough and play loud music.

---

1. What happened in the case?

2. What is the problem?

3. List everything the Deemers can do to solve the problem. Discuss the advantages and disadvantages to each solution.

4. Determine the two most workable solutions.

5. Suppose you suspect your neighbors of selling illegal drugs. Would you report them to the police? Give your reasons.

6. Suppose the Deemers constantly complain to the landlord, but nothing changes. Do you think the Deemers have the right to move out before the lease ends? Give your reasons.

THE HOME INSPECTION

Tenants have the right to **inspect** their new apartment before signing a lease or moving in. During an inspection, you and the landlord look at the apartment and make sure it is in good condition. Check to make sure everything works and is clean. This includes the lights, the heat, the stove, and the refrigerator. If anything needs repair, ask the landlord to repair it before you sign the lease.

YOUR TURN 25-2

INSPECTING THE APARTMENT

Read each question and follow the directions.

1. You are married and have two children. What things should you look for when inspecting an apartment?

2. What questions would you ask the landlord?

What to Inspect before Renting an Apartment

✔ What is the condition of the building?

✔ Are hallways, lobbies, and common areas clean and well lighted?

✔ Does the building have laundry facilities?

✔ Is there enough parking space?

✔ Are there any signs of insects or **rodents**?

✔ How are routine and emergency maintenance handled?

✔ Is storage and closet space adequate?

✔ Is the apartment soundproof?

✔ Are the plumbing, heating, and electrical fixtures in working order?

✔ Are kitchen appliances clean and in good condition?

✔ Is there any evidence of water stains or peeling paint on walls and ceilings?

✔ Does the building provide protection against burglars or uninvited guests?

✔ Is it likely to be cold in winter or too hot in the summer?

✔ Is the apartment furnished or unfurnished?

✔ Do windows and doors open easily?

✔ Are there any broken windows or screens?

✔ Are smoke detectors installed?

✔ Are fire extinguishers and safety exits available?

✔ Is the apartment big enough?

WHEN SOMETHING GOES WRONG

Tenants can do several things when something goes wrong in the apartment after they move in. As a tenant, you can:

1. **Complain to the landlord.** If you need the landlord to fix something, call or write the landlord to ask for the repair. If you call, keep a record of the date, the time, the person you talked to, and what the person said. If you write, keep a copy of the request. Then give the landlord time to take care of the problem. Most landlords do their best to make repairs. Their property is valuable to them.

2. **Repair and deduct.** In some states tenants can repair items in their apartment and subtract the cost from their next rent payment. They then give the landlord the remainder of the rent and the bill which proves they paid for the repair. If this is not allowed in your state, do not try it. The landlord may try to evict you for not paying rent. Then you'll have to prove in court that you told the landlord about the needed repair, that the landlord did not fix it, and that the repair was necessary.

3. **Complain to a government housing agency.** Many states and local governments have housing departments whose job it is to enforce **housing codes** or rules (see Figure 25-1). These housing codes set the **minimum** rules for safety and living conditions that a landlord must follow. If your apartment is not safe and does not have healthy living conditions, call the housing department. Tell them that you think your apartment is unsafe or unhealthy and that you want a housing inspector to look at it. The housing inspector will require your landlord to solve the problem. Housing codes have rules about plumbing, electricity, fire safety, room temperature, and rodents and insects.

4. **Stop paying rent.** Some states allow tenants to stop paying rent until the landlord makes needed repairs. This is a serious step that can get you evicted if your state does not allow rent withholding. Tenants should always talk with a lawyer before withholding rent.

5. **Sue the landlord.** If the landlord breaks the lease, the tenant may take the landlord to court. The tenant can ask the court to order the landlord to solve the problem. Some places have tenant-landlord commissions or small-claims courts that hear these types

◆ **FIGURE 25-1** SAMPLE HOUSING CODE

Sample Housing Code

The following are examples of provisions included in a typical housing code.

Maintenance and Repair

- Floors and walls shall be free of holes, cracks, splinters, or peeling paint.
- Windows and doors shall be weatherproof, easily operable, free of broken glass, and equipped with workable locks.
- Stairs and walkways shall be in good repair, clean, and free of safety hazards or loose railings.
- Roof shall be free of leaks.

Cleanliness and Sanitation

- Each unit shall be generally free of rodents and insects. Common areas shall be free of dirt, litter, trash, water, or other unsanitary matter.

Use and Occupancy

- Each unit shall have a minimum of 120 square feet of livable floor space per occupant.
- Each bedroom shall have a minimim of 50 square feet of floor space per occupant.
- Each unit shall have a private bathroom.
- Each common area shall be accessible without going through another apartment.

Facilities and Utilities

- Sinks, lavatories, and bathing facilities shall be in working order.
- Every room shall have a minimum of two electrical outlets and no exposed wiring.
- Water, electricity, gas, heating, and sewer services shall be in good operating condition.
- Halls, stairways, and common areas shall be adequately lighted.
- The building shall be free of fire hazards and secure from intruders or uninvited visitors.

of cases. These places do not require the tenant to hire a lawyer, so they do not cost as much as regular civil court.

6. **Move out of the apartment.**   If the place is not fit for you to live in, you may move out without telling the landlord in advance. This is a serious step. You must be able to prove that the apartment was unfit. Otherwise the landlord may sue you for the amount of rent money you owe from the time you move out until the end of the lease.

 YOUR TURN **25-3**

THE CASE OF THE RUN-DOWN APARTMENT

Read the following case. Decide what you would do.

> Mr. and Mrs. Walker rent an apartment. It has one bedroom. Rent is $250 a month. Mr. Martinez is the landlord. The apartment is dirty and run down. It is the only thing the Walkers can afford. Mr. and Mrs. Walker move in during the winter. The first week they discover the roof leaks. They also discover the apartment has roaches. The toilet always overflows, too. Three weeks after moving in, the heater stops. It is very cold at night. The Walkers are forced to stay with relatives for several days. Mr. Martinez never mentioned all these problems. The Walkers did not notice anything before they signed the lease.

1. Use the tenant action list to tell what the Walkers should do. Give your reasons.

2. Role-play a telephone call from the Walkers to Mr. Martinez.

3. If you were the landlord, what would you do?

4. The Walkers stop paying rent. Mr. Martinez takes them to court for not paying rent. Mr. Martinez asks the judge to require the Walkers to pay the rent owed and to evict them. You are the judge. What is your decision? Give your reasons.

Can you move out before the end of your lease?

MOVING OUT

What happens if you sign a lease, but want to move out before it ends? It depends. Most of the time you are still responsible for the rent until the end of the lease. However, if you or the landlord find a new renter, you may only have to pay for the time the apartment was unused.

YOUR TURN 25-4

MOVING OUT

Read the cases below and answer the questions.

1. Walden signs an apartment lease. It is for two years. Rent is $200 a month. After six months, Walden decides to get married. She wants to break the lease. She tells the landlord she is getting married.

    a. How much rent does Walden still owe?

    b. Is there anything Walden can do to break the lease and not pay the rent?

2. Wu signs an apartment lease. It is for one year. Rent is $300 a month. Before he moves in, he gives the landlord a $300 security deposit. After six months, Wu decides to move. He packs up his things and leaves. The landlord finds the apartment empty.

    a. How much rent does Wu still owe?

    b. What could Wu have done differently?

LESSON 26

You Are a Consumer

After this lesson you will be able to:

➤ define the terms *consumer* and *warranty*.
➤ explain actions which make a person a wise consumer.
➤ tell the purpose of consumer laws.
➤ give advice on actions to take when buying something.
➤ identify information which should be included in a warranty.
➤ write a letter of complaint.

WORDS TO KNOW

consumer – anyone who buys or uses goods or services *(noun)*

products – things that are made by someone to sell to other people *(noun)*

goods – products *(noun)*

estimate – guess; figure the approximate value of something *(verb)*

brands – products made by particular manufacturers or known by particular names *(noun)*

warranty – a promise that a product will work properly or the maker or seller will repair or replace it *(noun)*

guarantee – a promise to replace something sold if it does not work or last as it should *(noun)*

receipt – a written notice that payment was received for a product or service *(noun)*

defects – flaws in something; imperfections *(noun)*

freight – the cost paid to transport goods *(noun)*

commercial – having to do with business *(adjective)*

complaint – an expression of dissatisfaction or pain *(noun)*

model number – a number which tells the type or design of a product *(noun)*

serial number – an identification number *(noun)*

WHO IS A WISE CONSUMER?

You are a **consumer**. A consumer is anyone who buys or uses **products** and services. When you go to the dentist, ride on a bus, or have a television repaired, you are a consumer of services. When you buy food or clothes, you are a consumer of products. If you listen to the stereo or use the toaster, you are a consumer of products, too. You are a consumer, even if you don't buy the **goods** yourself.

What are some reasons a teen may want a car? What are some reasons a teen may need a car?

Anyone can be a wise consumer. Wise consumers think about whether they want or need a good or service. They know the difference between wanting something and needing something. Wise consumers don't spend so much money on things they want that they can't afford what they really need. They think about how they can pay for the product before making a purchase.

YOUR TURN 26-1

WANTS AND NEEDS

Read this case and answer the questions which follow.

> You just moved into an unfurnished apartment. The only things you brought with you were your clothes. This means you must purchase everything else you need and want. You have a job and take the bus to work. After paying rent, you have $500 left every month. You have saved $3,000.

1. List everything you *want* to buy before moving into the apartment.
2. List everything you *need* to buy before moving into the apartment.
3. **Estimate** the cost of each item from both lists.
4. Now make a list of what you will purchase. Only spend $3,000.
5. What would you do to find the actual cost of the items named?

BUYING A PRODUCT

Before Buying a Product or Service

✔ Compare prices by looking at different **brands** of the same item.

✔ Compare prices by shopping in more than one store, especially if the item is costly.

✔ Speak with friends to get recommendations about the product.

✔ Go to the library and read consumer magazines. These magazines tell you what to look for when buying the product and which products are best. Your librarian will help you locate the magazines.

✔ Read the **warranty** or **guarantee** carefully. A warranty is a promise that a product will work properly or the maker or seller will repair or replace it.

✔ Inspect the product. Look for anything that may be wrong. If the product is electric, plug it in before you leave the store.

Stores have different rules or policies. You should compare store policies. For example, a very low price at a store where all sales are final may not be a good deal if you buy a gift and don't know the exact size to buy. Store policies are usually written and placed where consumers can see them.

After buying the product, read and follow the instructions provided. Misuse of a product may be dangerous. It is also wise to save the **receipt** and the warranty. You will need the receipt if anything goes wrong with the product.

YOUR TURN 26-2

THE WARRANTY

Read the warranty below and answer the questions.

One-Year Warranty

Bright Electric Toothbrushes fully guarantees this product to the owner against **defects** in material and workmanship for one year from the date of purchase.

If the product does not work, mail it to the purchase place, approved service center, or Service Department, Bright Electric Toothbrushes, Inc., 3rd and Maple Streets, Arlington, PA 15616, **freight** prepaid, for free repair or replacement at our option.

Warranty does not include cost of inconvenience, damage due to product failure, transportation damages, misuse, abuse, accident, or **commercial** use.

For information, write Consumer Claims Manager at above Arlington address. Send owner's name, address, name of store or service center involved, model, serial number, purchase date, and description of problem.

This warranty gives certain legal rights. You may have other rights that vary from state to state.

This warranty becomes effective upon purchase.

To record the purchase date and to be sure you have warranty coverage, mail the enclosed registration card.

Your Turn **26-2** (continued)

1. What item is covered in this warranty?

2. Who will make any repairs?

3. What exactly is covered by the warranty?

4. What does the buyer have to do to start the warranty time?

5. What does the buyer have to do if the product needs repair during the warranted time?

CONSUMER LAWS

Sometimes even wise consumers have problems. Most business-people are honest, but sometimes businesspeople try to trick or cheat others. There are laws which protect anyone who buys or uses products and services. They are called consumer laws.

Consumer laws are written to protect consumers' rights as well as to protect honest businesses. Consumer laws are written by your local, state, and federal governments. Each of these governments has offices which deal with consumer problems and consumer laws. For example, there is a Consumer Affairs Office in the city of

What penalties should there be for dishonest business practices?

St. Louis which investigates consumer complaints. There is also a Consumer Affairs Office in the state of Missouri, and there is a Consumer Affairs Office which is run by the federal government. Any of the three offices may help when a consumer has a problem.

SOLVING CONSUMER PROBLEMS

Often, you can solve your own consumer problems. If you have a problem, try to contact the seller first. Many problems can be cleared up by talking to the seller. Be polite but firm. If that doesn't work, try writing a letter of **complaint** to the owner. If that doesn't work, contact and send a letter of complaint to the company that made the product. Ask your librarian to help you find the name of that company.

If you are still not satisfied, there are consumer agencies that can help you. Look in your telephone book in the blue pages or in the beginning of the white pages in the part called "Consumer Agencies." There you will find the names and phone numbers of agencies that can help you. One of the best-known consumer help agencies is the Better Business Bureau.

Finally, if you can't settle your complaint and a consumer agency has been unable to help, you may want to go to court and ask a judge to settle the dispute.

WRITING A LETTER OF COMPLAINT

The purpose of a letter of complaint is to get someone to agree with your side of an argument and to do something. Before the person to whom you are complaining can act, you must tell them what the problem is and what you want them to do. The most common mistake people make when writing letters of complaint is that they forget to tell the person to whom they are writing what action they want the person to take. Use the checklist on page 210 to make sure that your letters of complaint contain all the necessary information.

Consider mailing the letter from your post office and asking for a "return receipt." This will cost more than a regular stamp. A returned receipt is your proof that the company got your letter. The company may not ignore your letter if you can prove that the company received it.

Checklist for a Consumer Letter of Complaint

1. My name, address, and phone number

2. The person's name to whom I am writing

3. The address of the company to whom I am writing

4. My account number (if there is one)

5. Date of purchase of product

6. Place of purchase of product

7. **Model number** of product

8. **Serial number** of product

9. I explained the problem

10. I explained what I did about the problem

11. I stated what I want them to do about the problem

12. I stated when I want them to do something (be reasonable)

13. My handwriting or typing is clear

14. The letter is polite but firm

15. I included a *copy* of the receipt

16. I included a copy of other important papers

17. I have a copy of the letter

18. I mailed the letter

_____ } letterhead

_____ } dateline

_____
_____ } inside address
_____

_____ } salutation

_____ } body

_____ } complimentary close

_____ } signature

_____ } writer's name & identification

A consumer letter of complaint is a type of business letter. This is the style of a good business letter.

YOUR TURN **26-3**

A LETTER OF COMPLAINT

Read the story. Decide what you would do if you were the buyer.

> James Phillips bought a boom box from The Radio Shop and later tried to exchange it because it did not work. The date of the sale was November 14; the return was made ten days later. The bottom of the sales slip says, "This product is fully guaranteed for five days from the date of purchase. If defective, return it in the original box for credit toward another purchase."
> The store refused to make the exchange.

1. Role-play the meeting between the buyer and the seller in this story. What should the buyer say? What should the seller say?

2. Help James Phillips write a letter of complaint to the owner of the store. Use the checklist to make sure you include all of the information needed.

LESSON 27

Credit

After this lesson you will be able to:

> ➤ define credit.
> ➤ list advantages and disadvantages of using credit.
> ➤ discuss reasons for being approved for credit.
> ➤ discuss reasons for being denied credit.
> ➤ tell what to do if you are denied credit.

WORDS TO KNOW

credit – buying products or services with delayed payment or money that is loaned *(noun)*

finance charge – additional money owed to a lender for borrowing money *(noun)*

interest – money paid for the use of someone's money *(noun)*

annual – yearly *(adjective)*

co-sign – to sign a legal document promising to repay the money owed if the first signer does not pay; often a parent co-signs for an adult child *(verb)*

veteran's benefits – money the federal government pays to those who have served in the armed forces *(noun)*

Social Security – money the federal government pays to people when they retire *(noun)*

welfare – money the federal government pays to people in need *(noun)*

investigates – looks into or examines *(verb)*

minimum – the smallest amount or number that is possible *(adjective)*

insufficient – not enough *(adjective)*

WHAT IS CREDIT?

The use of **credit** is a way of life in the United States. Credit allows you to use goods, services, or money now and pay for them later. For example, credit lets you have a new pair of shoes, take a vacation, and have a car before you fully pay for them. You can borrow money and use the money to pay for such things as a house or a college education. Credit allows you to take advantage of sales and discounts. Even though credit is convenient and useful, making the monthly payments for the goods, services, and money can be expensive and difficult. Credit can tempt you to spend more money than you have. You can make wise choices if you learn about credit and think about how it should fit into your life.

When using credit, you must pay additional money to the people who lend you money or give you credit. For example, if you borrow one thousand dollars ($1,000) from the bank, you will need more than $1,000 to pay it back. The cost of credit is called a **finance charge**. This cost varies. It includes **interest** (money paid for the use of someone's money) and other fees. The more credit you receive, the greater the total finance charge. When you pay for goods purchased with credit, you pay money each month until you have paid for the item plus the finance charge.

The age you must be to get a credit card or take out a loan varies in different states. Some states' laws require you to be 18 years old, while other states' laws say you must be 21. No state allows you to borrow money on your own if you are younger than 18. Whom would you call to find out what the law is in your state?

Have you, your friends, or family members ever bought something on credit?

YOUR TURN 27-1

When Should You Use Credit?

Read the case below and think about whether Kayla should use credit.

> Kayla gets her first full-time job and moves to her first apartment. The only furniture she owns is a bed, a dresser, a kitchen table and chairs, and a television. She wants more furniture. Kayla looks in some furniture stores. Many of the stores offer furniture on credit. Kayla has saved $800, but does not want to use it all to buy furniture.

1. List reasons for Kayla using credit.

2. List reasons against Kayla using credit.

3. Role-play a conversation between Kayla and her friend, in which you discuss what Kayla should do about the furniture.

CREDIT CARDS

For many people, credit begins with the opening of a charge account. Some stores give you a credit card that is used only in their store. Other stores and banks have credit cards that are used in many places for many things including buying food, furniture, gasoline, or getting cash.

Stores, banks, and companies that issue credit cards charge you different amounts of money. Some places charge you an **annual** fee; others don't. An annual fee is money you pay each year for the right to use the credit card. If you are charged an annual fee, you must pay it every year, even if you do not use the credit card. Annual fees are usually between $15 and $75. All places that issue credit cards charge you interest, but interest rates vary.

Why is it important to read the credit agreement before signing it?

The federal Truth in Lending Act requires credit card companies to tell you the total amount of their finance charge, if you ask. Before you choose a credit card company, shop around to see what different companies charge for credit. Consider how much interest the company charges and if there is an annual fee.

APPLYING FOR A CREDIT CARD

When you apply for credit, both the credit card company and you have rights. The credit card company has a right to find out if you can pay back the money you borrow. You have the right to receive credit if you qualify for it.

You must fill out an application when applying for a credit card (see Figure 27-1 on page 218). A credit application asks for

◆ **FIGURE 27-1** A TYPICAL CREDIT APPLICATION

Credit Application

Please read the following before completing this form: (1) Applicant represents that the information given in this application is complete and accurate and authorizes us to check with credit reporting agencies, credit references and other sources disclosed herein in investigating the information given. (2) Applicant requests a credit card if our current consumer credit plan provides for the issuance of such a card. (3) Married applicants may apply for an individual account. READ AND SIGN THE ATTACHED AGREEMENT BEFORE SUBMITTING YOUR APPLICATION.

1. TELL US ABOUT YOURSELF *PLEASE PRINT*

First Name | Middle Initial | Last Name

Present Address | City | State | Zip Code

Previous Address (if less than two years at present address) | City | State | Zip Code

Birthdate / / | Social Security No. | Home Phone No. ( ) | Business Phone No. ( )

Employer | How Long (Years) | Annual Income* $ | Occupation: (✓)
1. ☐ Professional/Technical   4. ☐ Self-Employed
2. ☐ Sales   5. ☐ Retired
3. ☐ Clerical   6. ☐ Other

No. Dependents | ☐ Own ☐ Board ☐ Rent ☐ Live with Relatives | How Long (Years) | Mortgage/Rent Payment $

Credit References: (✓) ☐ Checking ☐ Savings ☐ VISA ☐ MasterCard ☐ Sears/Discover ☐ American Express/Optima ☐ Dept. Stores

2. PLEASE COMPLETE FOR CO-APPLICANT OR AUTHORIZED USER *Co-Applicant must sign Section 4 (Acknowledgement Signatures).*

First Name | Middle Initial | Last Name

Present Address | City | State | Zip Code

Annual Income* | Social Security No. | Relationship to Applicant ☐ Spouse ☐ Other | If individual listed above is Co-Applicant, check box ☐

3. INSURANCE OPTIONS
Indicate coverage chosen by signing and completing one of the following options. If insurance is not elected, do not sign or complete the following options.

By signing below, you acknowledge for any insurance elected that: (1) the purchase of such insurance was voluntary and was not required by us in the extension of credit; (2) the decision to purchase such insurance was made after we disclosed the cost of the insurance as set out in the agreement; and (3) you may obtain property insurance from a person of your own choosing other than us.

Single Credit Life, Disability, and Involuntary Unemployment Insurance with Property Insurance: ☐ is elected   ☐ is not elected

X

Buyer's Signature | Date | Age | Name of Proposed Insured (Accountholder or Accountholder's Spouse) | Age

4. ACKNOWLEDGEMENT SIGNATURE(S)

NOTICE TO BUYER: DO NOT SIGN BELOW BEFORE YOU HAVE RECEIVED AND READ THE COPY OF THE SELLER'S REVOLVING CREDIT ACCOUNT AGREEMENT.
You acknowledge that you have signed, dated, and kept the copy of the SELLER'S REVOLVING CREDIT ACCOUNT AGREEMENT and you agree to be bound by its terms and conditions.

SIGN HERE ▶ **X**
Buyer's Signature | Date | **X** Co-Buyer's Signature | Date

*Alimony, child support or separate maintenance payments need not be disclosed unless relied upon for credit.

Seller's Copy

FOR DEALER USE ONLY

Dealer Name | Telephone ( ) | Salesperson

Initial Amount Financed | Special Minimum Monthly Payment (applicable only if appropriate space on agreement is filled in) $ | Approval given by:

Branch No. | Dealer No. | Account No. | Credit Line

Do you have all the information to answer these questions now?

information about whether you can repay the money you owe. It also asks about your credit history. A credit history tells whether you repaid money you borrowed in the past. When credit card companies decide whether to give you credit, they want to know about your credit history.

WHAT IS IN YOUR CREDIT REPORT?

Credit reports contain information about your:

1. **ABILITY TO REPAY** Credit card companies want to know if you have a job and how much you earn. They want to know how much money is in your savings account. The company needs to make sure you have enough money to pay it after you have paid your other bills. It may require someone with a good credit record to **co-sign** for the credit card. That person must agree to pay the bill if you do not pay it.

2. **DEPENDABILITY** Credit card companies want to know how long you have worked at your job and the length of time you have lived at your current address. They want to make sure that you are dependable and do not change jobs or move frequently.

3. **CREDIT HISTORY** Credit card companies ask you to list all your bills, how much you owe each month, and the total amount due. Before issuing you credit, the company considers whether you pay your bills on time. It is difficult to get a credit card if you have no credit history.

4. **PROPERTY** Credit card companies want to know if you own a car, a house, or things that can be sold to pay what you owe.

The law requires credit card companies to treat those who apply for credit fairly. The federal Equal Credit Opportunity Act says that a company which issues credit may not refuse you credit, if you qualify. The law does not guarantee that you will get credit. It says companies must follow the same rules for everyone with similar income, bills, and credit history.

Companies Cannot Deny You Credit Based on:

✔ race

✔ color

✔ age

✔ sex

✔ country of birth

✔ marital status

✔ whether or not you receive public income, such as **veteran's benefits**, **Social Security**, or **welfare**.

 YOUR TURN **27-2**

TO WHOM WOULD YOU ISSUE A CREDIT CARD?

Imagine that you own a credit card company. The four people described below have filled out applications for credit. Would you issue them credit cards? Give your reasons.

1. Jerry is a carpenter who receives veteran's benefits and works whenever he can. Because of the weather, he cannot always find jobs.

2. Alice quit her job to go back to school to become a doctor. Even though she saved a lot of money, she knows she may not always have enough to pay her bills. Alice got her parents to agree to co-sign her credit card application.

3. Martin just lost his factory job. Until recently, he paid his rent and bills, but now he does not have enough money to pay for everything.

4. Stella used to own a car, but the car dealer took it back because she did not make her car payments when they were due. She promises to pay on time if you issue her a credit card.

WHAT HAPPENS AFTER YOU APPLY FOR CREDIT?

After you apply for credit, the credit company **investigates** you. The company pays a credit bureau to check your credit record. A credit bureau is a business that collects information about you, such as your address, what bills you owe, and your bill-paying practices. This information is called a credit report. Credit bureaus do not make credit decisions. They give credit reports to credit companies, and the credit company decides whether or not to give you credit.

Credit bureaus use computers to keep information about your credit history. Look under "Credit Reporting Agencies" in the yellow pages of your telephone book to find names of credit bureaus in your area.

APPROVAL OF CREDIT

Credit card companies must tell you if your credit card application was approved or denied within 30 days after you apply for credit.

If your credit is approved, the credit company will send you a credit card with your name and account number on it. You are responsible for paying the bills and for protecting your credit card. The credit card allows you to purchase goods and services until you reach a certain amount of credit. This is called your credit limit. Each month the company sends you a statement telling you how much you owe. Most credit card companies allow you to pay the bill over time and pay the smallest or **minimum** payment each month. It is wise to pay as much as you can to avoid paying a lot of money in interest.

 YOUR TURN **27-3**

UNDERSTANDING A CREDIT CARD BILL

Examine the sample credit card bill and answer the questions that follow.

UNITED VIRGINIA BANK CARD STATEMENT
P.O. BOX 56432   MINNEAPOLIS, MN 55549-0321

Joan Q. Consumer
100 Main Street
Anywhere, USA

STATEMENT CLOSING DATE:
2/12/99

CUSTOMER SERVICE
1-800-777-6302

MAIL PAYMENT BY	TO ENSURE IT IS RECEIVED BY	ACCOUNT NUMBER	
3-01-99	3-08-99	4366-040-878-000	
BILLING DATE	CREDIT LIMIT		CREDIT AVAILABLE
2-08-99	$1,000.00		$655.83

TRANSACTION DATE	BILLING DATE	TRANSACTION DESCRIPTION		AMOUNT
01-07	01-18	Dodge State Park	Ft Wayne, IN	$ 30.03
01-03	01-25	Economy Hotel	Ashville, NC	39.71
02-02	02-02	—PAYMENT—	THANK YOU	100.00
01-27	02-08	Thrifty Motel	South Hill, VA	34.51
02-05	02-09	Snap Shot Camera	Washington, DC	87.67

PREVIOUS BALANCE	PAYMENTS	NEW PURCHASES	FINANCE CHARGE	NEW BALANCE
250.00	100.00	191.92	2.25	344.17

DATE DUE	MINIMUM PAYMENT
3-08-99	10.00

1. What is Joan Q. Consumer's finance charge for this month?

2. What is her new balance?

3. How did the United Virginia Bank figure out this new balance?

4. When is her next payment due?

5. What is the minimum amount she can pay?

Protect Your Credit Card

1. Sign your new credit card as soon as it arrives to prevent someone else from using it.

2. Open and check your monthly bill as soon as it arrives. Make sure all charges belong to you. Call or write the bank to report any questionable charges. The bank usually provides a toll free—800 or 888—telephone number.

3. Keep a list of your credit card numbers and the phone numbers for reporting lost or stolen cards. Report lost or stolen cards immediately. If a thief uses your card before you report it missing, you may owe $50. If a thief uses your card after you report it missing, you owe nothing.

4. Never give your credit card number over the phone, unless you make the call.

DENIAL OF CREDIT

If your credit report shows that you are a poor risk, you will probably be denied credit. The Equal Credit Opportunity Act requires companies to tell you, in writing, exactly why you were turned down. For example, "does not meet our standards" is not exact enough. However, "**insufficient** income" is exact enough.

The Fair Credit Reporting Act protects you against incorrect or out-of-date information being reported about you in credit bureau reports. If you are denied credit because of something in a credit report, the company must tell you the name, address, and phone number of the credit bureau that provided the report. Then you can call, write, or visit the credit bureau to ask for a copy of the report.

You are allowed to receive one copy of your credit report free if you have been denied credit within the last 60 days. If the information on the report is wrong, you can give the credit bureau the correct information. Then the credit bureau must prove that what they reported is true. To find out if the credit bureau has corrected the information, you need to request another copy of the report.

Information stays on your credit report for seven years; then it is removed.

YOUR TURN 27-4

WHAT TO DO IF YOU ARE DENIED CREDIT

1. Read the examples below and decide whether each one is a fair or an unfair reason to deny credit.

   a. "You do not have a good job."

   b. "We do not give credit cards to people born outside the U.S."

   c. "You have a history of not paying your bills on time."

   d. "You do not have any credit history at all."

2. Sam was denied credit. The letter he received from his bank said that he was not a good risk because he had moved five times in the last five years. The information is wrong. Sam lived at only one address. He wants to correct the report that the Ames Credit Bureau sends out. Role-play a conversation between Sam and the person answering the phone at Ames Credit Bureau.

3. Write a letter to the Ames Credit Bureau from Sam. Tell the company about the phone conversation and correct its wrong information.

LESSON 28

Buying a Car

After this lesson you will be able to:

➤ list some things to consider before buying a car.
➤ explain some advertising laws which help car buyers.
➤ name an advantage and a disadvantage of buying a new car.
➤ name an advantage and a disadvantage of buying a used car.
➤ explain the difference between buying a car with a warranty and an "as is" car.
➤ explain some consumer protection laws which help car buyers.

WORDS TO KNOW

make – a brand or type of car *(noun)*

model – a style or design *(noun)*

manual transmission – a gearbox in a car or truck that requires the driver to shift gears by pushing the clutch down by foot while shifting gears by hand *(noun)*

automatic transmission – a gearbox in a car or truck that shifts gears as the vehicle goes faster without the driver operating the gears *(noun)*

trade-in – something such as a car which is turned in as payment or part-payment for a purchase *(noun)*

minor – a person who is under the age for being an adult according to law *(noun)*

bill of sale – a document showing the terms of purchase *(noun)*

defects – flaws in something; imperfections *(noun)*

full warranty – a promise to repair the sold item or replace it free of charge if something goes wrong within an indicated amount of time *(noun)*

limited warranty – a promise to repair or replace certain parts of a sold item if something goes wrong, including restrictions on what part or parts and the time frame *(noun)*

odometer – instrument in a motor vehicle recording the mileage it has been driven *(adjective)*

BEFORE YOU BUY A CAR

One of your first and most expensive major purchases may be a car. Many things influence your decision about what car is best for you. Automobile magazines that put the latest model sports car on their covers have a different opinion from consumer magazines about what car is best. One may emphasize how cars look and how you feel while driving the car. The other may emphasize safety features and the price of the car. All of these things may be important to you. Buying a car is often hard to do.

What kind of car will you buy?

 YOUR TURN **28-1**

CHOOSING YOUR CAR

1. List all the things you must consider before buying a car.

2. Compare your list with the one on page 228. How are the lists alike? How are they different?

3. What are the advantages and disadvantages of buying a new car?

4. What are the advantages and disadvantages of buying a used car?

Some Things to Consider before Buying a Car

✔ Why do I need the car?

✔ Do I want a new or used car?

✔ What **make** and **model** car do I want?

✔ What features must the car have (example: air conditioning)?

✔ How much money can I afford to pay?

✔ How much will car insurance cost?

✔ What are repair costs for cars like the one I want?

✔ How much will taxes and car registration cost?

✔ Where can I find the car?

✔ What is the warranty on the car?

✔ How will I use this car?

✔ Do I want a car with **manual transmission** or **automatic transmission**?

✔ Do I have a **trade-in**? How much can I get for it?

In Detroit, where some cars are made, they say, "A car is fashion: the sheet-metal sport jacket." Explain what that means.

NEW OR USED CAR?

There are advantages and disadvantages to buying both new and used cars. One advantage of buying a new car is that the car is likely to be in good condition. A disadvantage is that new cars are expensive. You are required to have a high down payment or trade-in and you will probably make monthly payments for three to five years.

More than half of the people who buy cars purchase used ones. One advantage of buying used cars is they are cheaper than new ones. A disadvantage is you may get a car that needs repairs and doesn't run well. No matter if you purchase a new or used car, there are laws to protect you, the buyer.

ADVERTISING FOR CARS

There are advertisements for new and used cars in newspapers, on the radio, and on television. The Federal Trade Commission and your state consumer protection agency regulate most laws about advertisements. Car advertisements must follow the same laws as other advertisements. Many laws about advertisements were written because car ads are particularly troublesome. These laws vary from state to state. In some states, a dealer's car ad must include the number of available cars of that type. In other states, dealer car ads must include the price and what features come with the advertised car.

Some Laws about Car Advertisements

✔ A dealer or seller cannot advertise a car at a low price, and then tell you that model is sold out and try to sell you a higher-priced car. This is called "bait and switch." It is against the law.

✔ A seller cannot say a car is new, if it is used. The answer to the question, "What is a used car?" varies from state to state. Some states say a car is used if it was driven more than the distance necessary to deliver a new car to the dealer and to test-drive it. Other states say a car is used if it was driven over a certain number of miles. For example, in Maryland, a car is used if it was driven over 6,000 miles.

YOUR TURN **28-2**

READING CAR ADS

Read the ads and answer the questions that follow.

1. FORD—'85 Tempo, 5 speed, 2 door, air conditioned, am/fm radio
   & cassette, power steering, power brakes, sunroof. 1 owner.
   Needs work. $1,500 or best offer. Call 444-2233

   a. What information is not included in this ad?
   b. What questions would you ask if you called about the ad?
   c. Imagine you are interested in buying this car. Role-play the
      conversation you would have with the person who placed the ad.

2. HONDA—'82 Civic, am/fm radio, air conditioned, new tires,
   repainted, 150,000 miles, runs great. $1,200. Call 333-4422

   a. What information is not included in this ad?
   b. What questions would you ask if you called about the ad?
   c. Imagine you are trying to sell this car. Role-play the conversation
      you would have with someone interested in buying it.

3. Tyler and his sister, Tracy, are shopping for a used car. They see
   an ad in the Friday newspaper that says, "Come to Betsy's Bargain
   Cars for the best car deals in town. This weekend only, all compact
   cars reduced in price." When they arrive at Betsy's Bargain Cars,
   the salesperson tells them that their compact cars are not in very
   good condition. She suggests that they look at a nicer car that is
   not reduced but that will last longer. The nicer car costs at least
   $1,000 more than the compacts.

   a. Role-play the conversation between Tyler, Tracy, and the
      salesperson.
   b. Has the salesperson used bait-and-switch advertising, or was
      she just looking out for Tyler and Tracy? Give your reasons.
   c. What is the best way to handle a salesperson if the person tries
      to bait-and-switch you?

4. Select three car ads from the newspaper. What questions would
   you ask if you called about the ads?

WHO CAN BUY A CAR

A young person who has not yet reached the age of adulthood, usually 18 or 21 years of age, is called a **minor**. A minor cannot be forced to carry out promises and may cancel or refuse to follow a contract. Buying a car is a contract between the buyer and the seller, even if no one writes or signs something. If a minor buys a car, the seller will ask the parents to sign the **bill of sale**.

WHERE TO LOOK FOR A CAR

A car dealer, according to the law, is someone who sells six or more cars in a 12-month period. Some new cars are sold by dealers

Why do you think they are called car "dealers"?

who sell varieties of the same make. For example, a Ford dealer may sell the Ford Bronco, the Ford Taurus, and the Ford Escort. After choosing the model of car you want, go to a dealer that carries that make of car.

Used cars are sold in a variety of places. There are two kinds of used-car dealers. One sells new and used cars. The other sells only used cars. Used-car dealers who sell both new and used cars offer more expensive cars. These dealers often have repair shops where the car is repaired before it is sold. The repair shop is available if anything goes wrong with the car later. Dealers who sell only used cars can offer lower prices, but many do not have repair shops available if something goes wrong. Rental agencies also sell used cars. Many used cars are sold by private sellers.

Whether to buy a used car from a dealer or a private seller is your choice. Go with whomever gives you the best deal and with whom you are the most comfortable. Some experts believe you are better off buying from a private seller. They think a private seller will give you a more accurate description of the car's faults, based on personal knowledge. They believe you get a lower price from a private seller. However, private sellers seldom give warranties, which dealers sometimes offer. Other experts believe you are better off with a dealer because you have a better chance of getting help if something goes wrong. Most states have laws about used-car sales that apply only to used-car dealers.

You can locate new- and used-car dealers by looking in the yellow pages of the phone book. You can also look under "Automobiles" in the classified section of newspapers. You can locate dealers and private sellers there. If you want to buy a used car from a private seller, you might start by asking friends if they know anyone who wants to sell his or her car.

YOUR TURN 28-3

CARMEN AND THE CAR

Read the following story. Answer the questions that follow.

Carmen can afford to spend about $2,500 for a car. After looking for several weeks, she finds a used car she likes at Dealer Dan's. She test-drives it and looks it over carefully with her family's mechanic. The mechanic tells her that the car needs $150 of work to make it run well. Dealer Dan is asking $3,000 for the car. Carmen really wants this car.

Dealer Dan's job is to sell cars so that he can make enough money to cover his expenses, including what he paid for the cars and what it takes to run his dealership, and make some money to live on. Dan paid $2,000 for the car. Dan's Dealership has a repair shop which could do all the work Carmen's mechanic said the car needs. Dan really wants to sell Carmen this car.

1. If you were Carmen, what would you say or do to get Dealer Dan to lower the price of the car?

2. What is the highest price Carmen should pay for the car?

3. If you were Dealer Dan, what would you say or do to get Carmen to pay full price for the car?

4. What is the lowest price Dealer Dan should receive for the car?

5. If you were Carmen, what would make you decide to go elsewhere for a car, even though you like this one?

WARRANTY AND "AS IS" CARS

All new cars and some used ones have a warranty. A warranty is a guarantee or promise made by the seller that any **defects** arising during the time period of the warranty will be fixed by the seller. There are two kinds of warranties, limited and full. A **full warranty** agrees that defects will be repaired within a certain period of time and without charge. In a full warranty everything is covered. A **limited warranty** may require that you pay for labor when defective parts are replaced or that you pay for items such as belts, hoses, and filters. Most cars with a warranty, including new ones, have a limited warranty. The law requires that sellers label warranties as either "limited" or "full."

The Federal Trade Commission now requires used-car dealers to place a large sticker called a Buyer's Guide in the window of every car, van, or truck offered for sale. The sticker must tell whether the vehicle comes with a warranty. If so, the sticker must tell you what the warranty includes. The sticker advises you to get all promises in writing and to have the car inspected by a mechanic before you buy it. Private sellers are not required to display the Buyer's Guide sticker.

Many people sell used cars "as is." This means the car comes without a warranty or promise about how the car will perform. By taking the car as is, you accept it in whatever condition it is in. If the car needs repairs, it is your responsibility to pay for them.

LEMON LAWS

Most states have lemon laws that keep you from getting stuck with a new car that keeps breaking down no matter how many times it has been in the shop. Under these laws, you are usually entitled to a refund or a replacement car if your new car cannot be fixed in four tries, or if the car is out of service 30 days within the first 12,000 miles or 12 months.

Give a reason why the federal government requires used-car dealers to have a Buyer's Guide sticker on the car window.

A growing number of states have lemon laws that cover used cars. In some places the law applies to both dealers and private sellers. These laws usually protect you when two conditions occur: 1) if the car fails a state safety inspection within a certain time from the date of sale, and 2) if repair costs are higher than a stated percentage of the purchase price; for example, if you pay $800 for a car and two weeks later you discover that you must pay $2,000 to repair it.

If a car is covered by a used-car lemon law, you can cancel the deal within a certain time period. You must write the seller and say that you intend to cancel the deal. You must give your reasons. Next you must return the car to the place of sale, even if it requires towing.

For information about lemon laws in your state, contact your state consumer protection agency or attorney general's office.

OTHER CONSUMER PROTECTION LAWS FOR CAR BUYERS

Safety features are important because, in an average year, one out of every three drivers has an automobile accident!

SAFETY INSPECTIONS

Most states require that cars pass a safety inspection before a car sale is final. A new car should easily pass inspection. Someone other than the dealer should inspect a used car. State inspections vary, but most inspect the car's lights, brakes, windshield wipers, horn, and seat belts. What is inspected in your state's car safety inspections?

CAR MILEAGE

Federal law entitles a car buyer to receive a statement giving the **odometer** reading on the car. An odometer is the equipment that shows the number of miles a car has been driven. The buyer must request the statement. Refusal to provide a statement or changing the odometer reading are both against the law. This law is called the federal Anti-Odometer Law.

UNFAIR SALES PRACTICES

Laws vary but many states have laws that make it illegal for a seller to deceive or lie to you about the car he or she is selling. Sellers cannot hide dangerous defects from you or hide important facts about the car's past use from you. For example, the seller must tell you if the car was in an accident requiring the engine to be replaced.

 YOUR TURN 28-4

THE CASE OF THE USED-CAR PURCHASE

Read these cases and answer the questions that follow.

1. Jillian bought a used car from Mr. Green, who said that the car had never been wrecked. Later a mechanic told Jillian that the car had been in a major accident. Did Mr. Green break any laws? Give your reasons.

2. Beverly bought a used car from Gold Used-Car Dealership. It had 60,000 miles on it. Mr. Gold mailed Beverly her car title. The title said that the car had 150,000 miles on it. Were any laws broken? Give your reason.

3. Paul sold his car to his friend, Leon. Leon knows that the car rarely runs and is paying only $50 for it. The car runs for one week and then stops. Were any laws broken? Give your reason.

4. Jackie has taken her new car back for service five times in two months. Can Jackie get another car? Give your reasons.

LESSON 29

Serving on a Jury

As a result of this lesson, you will be able to:
- ➤ explain what a juror does and why it's important.
- ➤ describe how jurors are selected.
- ➤ complete a juror selection questionnaire.
- ➤ explain who can serve on a jury.

 **WORDS TO KNOW**

juror – a member of a jury *(noun)*

evidence – facts or things used to prove something in court *(noun)*

jury – a group of people who are chosen to listen to facts and evidence in a trial and decide the outcome of the case *(noun)*

peers – people of the same worth; equals *(noun)*

utility – a useful service or product such as water, gas, electricity, or telephone service provided to the public *(noun)*

questionnaire – a list of questions used in gathering information from people *(noun)*

summons – an order to appear somewhere or to do something *(noun)*

visual – having to do with seeing *(adjective)*

sign language interpreters – people who use hand movements, instead of spoken words, to talk *(noun)*

THE JOB

A Riddle

My job is more important than the judge's job.

I decide who wins the case.

Who am I?

If you guessed **juror**, you are right. The job of a juror is to listen to facts and **evidence** in a trial and decide which side is right. This job is important because juries enable those who are on trial to be judged by a "**jury** of their **peers**". Peers are people who are similar to you. For example, people the same age as you may be your peers.

The right to a jury is guaranteed by the Sixth and Seventh Amendments to the Constitution. Juries make the Constitution work. People serve on juries because it is their responsibility as citizens. Imagine how you would feel if you were involved in a case and wanted to have a jury trial, but no one wanted to serve.

◆ **FIGURE 29-1**   JUROR QUALIFICATION FORM

JUROR QUALIFICATION FORM*

Please read and print your answers to the questions below.

1.   Are you a citizen of the United States?   YES☐   NO☐

2.   Are you now and for the last six months a resident of   YES☐   NO☐
     Washington, New York?

3.   Are you 18 years of age or older?   YES☐   NO☐

4.   Can you speak and understand the English language?   YES☐   NO☐

5.   Do you have any physical or mental handicap that would
     not permit you to serve as a juror?   YES☐   NO☐

6.   Have you served as a juror within the last two years?   YES☐   NO☐

7.   Do you have a pending felony or misdemeanor charge
     in any federal or state court?   YES☐   NO☐

8a.   Have you ever been convicted of a felony?   YES☐   NO☐

8b.   If the answer to 8a was yes, was it more than 10 years ago?   YES☐   NO☐

Juror's Name:_____

Juror's Address:_____

Age:_____   Sex:_____   M_____   F_____

Employer:_____

_____

*Adapted from the juror qualification form used in the Superior Court of the District of Columbia.

JURY SELECTION

For many adults, voting and serving on juries are the two main ways they participate in government. Juries are made up of people from the community. Court officials first select the names of possible jurors from such places as voter registration lists, driver's license registration lists, the telephone book, and **utility** user lists. After selecting the names, officials send the possible juror a **questionnaire** (see Figure 29-1 on page 239). The law requires the possible juror to answer and return the questionnaire.

YOUR TURN 29-1

SAMPLE JUROR QUESTIONNAIRE

Read about Rhonda. On a separate piece of paper, answer the questions on the questionnaire as if you were Rhonda.

> Rhonda Gomes is a 19-year-old U.S. citizen who lives at 3825 Tara Lane in Washington, New York. She was born in Washington and graduated from Eastern High School. Rhonda attended special education classes and did not learn to read very well. She has had several speeding tickets and has had her driver's license suspended. Rhonda has never been in any other trouble with the law. This is the first time Rhonda has filled out a questionnaire like this.

After officials review the returned questionnaires, they make a list of people qualified to serve on a jury. Those qualified receive a court paper, called a **summons** (see Figure 29-2), which orders the possible juror to come to court.

◆ **FIGURE 29-2** SUMMONS FOR JURY SERVICE

SUMMONS FOR JURY SERVICE

Office of the Clerk of the Court
Superior Court of Freedom County
500 Main Avenue
Washington, NY 23456

Name: Rhonda Gomes

Address: 3825 Tara Ln.

     Washington, NY 27654

Subject: SUMMONS FOR JURY SERVICE

By the order of the Chief Judge of the Superior Court of Freedom County, you
are hereby summoned to serve as a juror as indicated below. Failure to appear as
directed by this summons may result in a fine of not more than three hundred
dollars ($300) or imprisonment for not more than seven (7) days or both.
F.C. Code 11-1907.

Date and Time to Report: *Type of Jury:*
February 1, 1999   Petit Jury
    9:00 A.M.

Where to Report: *Length of Service:*
Superior Court of Freedom County   One Trial
500 Main Street
Washington, NY
Room 213   Signed,

_____
Clerk of Court

_____
Chief Judge

*Adapted from the juror qualification form used in the Superior Court of the District of Columbia.

YOUR TURN 29-2

JURY SUMMONS

Read the jury summons on page 241 for Rhonda Gomes and answer the questions below.

1. Where should Rhonda report?

2. What time should she report there?

3. How long does Rhonda need to be available?

4. What will happen if Rhonda does not report to court?

5. If Rhonda gets sick on the day she is to report for duty, what should she do?

WHO MAY SERVE

You may serve on a jury if you live in the United States or the state where the trial is held, are 18 years old or older, and have not been convicted of a felony.

YOUR TURN 29-3

BLIND JURORS

In many states and in Washington, D.C., court officials do not allow any citizen who is blind to serve on a jury. There was a court case to have this practice changed. Read each side of the case and be prepared to discuss how you feel about the issue.

Blind Citizens Should Not Serve on Juries

Blind citizens should not be allowed to serve on juries. Sometimes there is evidence a juror needs to see. Many times, an attorney will have charts to show the jury such things as where an accident happened. The attorney may have pictures of a crime scene. A blind juror will not be able to see the evidence. That will be unfair to whichever side gives the evidence.

Also, sometimes a juror can look at a person and tell if he or she is believable. For example, suppose a witness says that the defendant in a murder case was with him the night of the crime. While the witness is talking, he smiles and winks at the defendant. A blind juror would not see this.

I think it will be unfair to both sides if blind citizens are allowed to serve on juries.

Blind Citizens Should Serve on Juries

Blind citizens should be allowed to serve on juries. There are many trials in which there is no **visual** evidence presented at the trial. A good juror is a good listener. It is important that a juror hear witnesses, not see them. Court decisions should be based on what witnesses say, not how they look. If a witness is not telling the truth, it is the job of the attorney to prove it.

Citizens who are deaf or hard of hearing serve on juries, so why is it different for people who are blind? The court provides people who are deaf with **sign language interpreters** to help them perform as jurors. Why do we treat citizens who are blind differently?

I think preventing blind citizens from serving on a jury is against the law. The law says that the government cannot treat someone differently just because the person has a disability. This law is called the Americans with Disabilities Act. It is not right if the government breaks its own laws.

LESSON 30

Voting

After this lesson you will be able to:

> ➤ explain the purpose of voting.
> ➤ list the constitutional guidelines states must follow when deciding who can vote.
> ➤ list typical state guidelines about who may and who may not vote in government elections.
> ➤ define and tell the purpose of voter registration.

 ## WORDS TO KNOW

election – the act of making a choice *(noun)*

polls – places where people go to vote in an election *(noun)*

qualified – having the skill, experience, or fit that is needed *(adjective)*

ballot – a piece of paper on which a person marks her or his choice in voting *(noun)*

absentee ballots – ballots used to vote without being physically there *(noun)*

dishonorably discharged – released from the armed services in disgrace *(adjective)*

register – to enter your name into an official record as being qualified to vote; a requirement for voting *(verb)*

WHAT IS VOTING?

Voting is one way people make a choice and express their wishes. You have voted many times. Sometimes you vote by raising your hand; other times you write your choice on a piece of paper; and sometimes you vote by saying yes or no. This was an **election**. After you choose, someone counts your choices. Usually the most votes win. What have you voted for or against? Where were you when you voted?

In our government, voting is the way we choose the people we want to run the government. You vote by going to special places called **polls**. When you get to the poll, there are either ballot boxes or voting machines. You either put your vote in the ballot box or record your vote on the voting machine.

Why are voting machines more secure than ballot boxes?

 YOUR TURN 30-1

WHO VOTES FOR STUDENT COUNCIL PRESIDENT?

1. Imagine your school is going to vote for president of the student council. The principal picks you and two other students to make sure that only those who are **qualified** vote. The following people want to vote. Decide if you will let them. Give your reasons.

   a. Shanika attends your school. She is a "B" student and wants to vote.

   b. Sean attends another high school, but he knows someone running for president and wants to vote.

Your Turn   **30-1** (continued)

    c. Elizabeth attends your school. She is really different; her hair is green. Elizabeth wants to vote.

    d. Peter's first day at this school is today. He has not met anyone at the school and doesn't know who is running for president. Peter wants to vote.

    e. Margaret attends your school. She is blind and can't see the **ballot**, but Margaret wants to vote.

    f. Louis attends your school. He cannot read, but he wants to vote.

    g. Kim attends your school, but she is at home sick. Kim will not be well before the election, but she wants to vote.

    h. Jon attends your school, but he will not be there on election day because he was suspended. Jon wants to vote.

2. Write a rule that lists the requirements for voting in the school election.

WHO CAN VOTE?

Just as you made rules about who could vote in the school election above, each state makes laws about who can vote in its state. The laws in states are similar because all states must follow certain basic guidelines. These guidelines were set by the U.S. Constitution and by decisions of the U.S. Supreme Court.

Constitutional Guidelines for Voting

1. Any person who votes in state elections may also vote in federal elections.

2. No state can deny persons the right to vote because of their race or color.

3. No state can deny persons the right to vote because they are females or males.

4. No state can deny the right to vote because of age if a person is 18 years of age or older.

5. No state can require a voter to pay a tax before voting.

Today each state requires voters to live within that state before they can vote. Some states require you to live there 30 days, while others only require voters to prove they live in the state.

Until 1971, states required voters to live there a much longer period of time. One such state was Tennessee. Tennessee required people to live in the state for one year before the person could vote. The Supreme Court decided that the law discriminated against people who move to Tennessee. The Supreme Court said that 30 days seems to be enough time to require people to live in the state before they can vote.

All states require that you be a citizen of the United States before you can vote. You are a citizen if you were born in the United States or if you were made a citizen by law.

All states allow most people with disabilities to vote. The law says that polls must be usable by everyone. If the poll cannot be used by a person with a disability, the state must find a way for that person to vote. What do you think these methods are? Most states have **absentee ballots** and curbside voting for people with disabilities.

WHO CANNOT VOTE?

Every state denies the vote to certain people. No state allows people in mental hospitals or people whom the law says are mentally unfit to vote. Nearly all states deny the vote to persons who have been convicted of a felony. Some states deny the right to vote to the homeless. Some states also deny the vote to persons who have been **dishonorably discharged** from the armed services.

 YOUR TURN **30-2**

VOTING FREEDOM

1. Following are two sample concept maps. On a separate sheet of paper, complete each concept map using the list below. On one map, write the matching types of people around "People Who May Vote in a Government Election." On the other map, write the matching types of people around "People Who May Not Vote in a Government Election."

Your Turn **30-2** (continued)

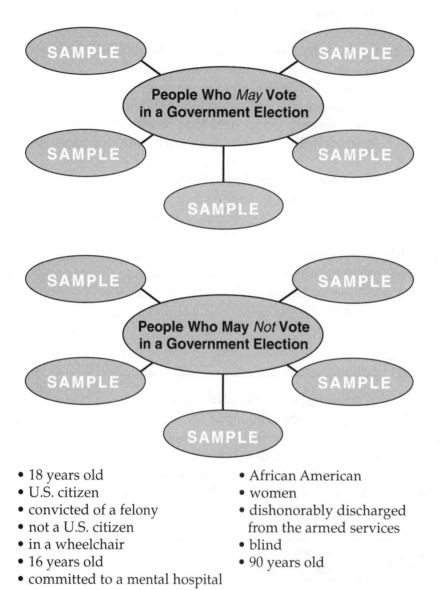

- 18 years old
- U.S. citizen
- convicted of a felony
- not a U.S. citizen
- in a wheelchair
- 16 years old
- committed to a mental hospital

- African American
- women
- dishonorably discharged
  from the armed services
- blind
- 90 years old

2. Imagine you live in the state of Freedom. It is one of the United States, so you must follow the guidelines of the Constitution and the decisions of the Supreme Court. Tell if the following people can register to vote in the state of Freedom. Give your reasons.

a. Mr. O'Brien is a 16-year-old U.S. citizen who lives in Freedom. He has lived there all of his life.

b. Ms. Bond is a 30-year-old U.S. citizen. She has lived in Freedom for six months.

c. Mr. Zimmer is a 30-year-old U.S. citizen who lives in Freedom. He was just released from prison. Mr. Zimmer was convicted of rape.

d. Mrs. Kulski is an 80-year-old citizen who lives in a nursing home in Freedom.

e. Mr. Gomez is 50 years old. He moved to Freedom from Mexico several years ago. He is not a U.S. citizen.

f. Ms. Blue is a 25-year-old citizen who lives in Freedom. She was dishonorably discharged from the army.

g. Mr. Olsen is a 42-year-old citizen who lives in Freedom. He was convicted of shoplifting a pair of jeans.

h. Ms. Rosen is a 21-year-old citizen who lives in the Freedom State Mental Hospital. She is a patient.

VOTER REGISTRATION

In all states except North Dakota, you must **register** before you can vote. This means your name must be on a list of qualified

Where and how can people register to vote in your state?

voters. To get your name on the list of registered voters, you must fill out a voter registration form which usually asks your name, address, place of birth, and where you live. One job of election officials is to make it easy for people to register to vote. More than half of the states now allow voter registration through the mail. Most states also provide for voter registration at their Department of Motor Vehicles. Sometimes, voter registrars even go door-to-door to register voters.

Some say that more people would vote if they didn't have to register first. They want to do away with the registration requirement. Others say that registering guarantees that only people who are qualified get to vote. In the country of South Africa, millions of people voted for the first time without registering. South Africans came to the polls on election day with proof of who they were. After voting, an election official stamped voters' hands so they couldn't vote twice. Do you think that would work in this country? Give your reasons.

Glossary

Absentee ballots   ballots used to vote without being physically there *(noun)*

Abuse   mistreatment *(noun)*

Accent   a special way of pronouncing words *(noun)*

Accommodation   an adjustment that meets a need *(noun)*

Achievement tests   tests you take in school that tell what you know *(noun)*

Advertise   to call public attention to *(verb)*

Advice   opinion given as to what to do *(noun)*

Aggravated assault   a very serious use of force or a physical attack *(noun)*

Annual   yearly *(adjective)*

Appealed   made an earnest request *(verb)*

Appliances   machines made for a particular use in a house or office, like a fan or a refrigerator *(noun)*

Application   a request *(noun)*

Appoint   to name or choose to represent you *(verb)*

Aptitude   a natural ability; talent *(noun)*

Arguments   reasons for disagreement between two or more parties presented to a judge *(noun)*

Attitude   a way of acting or behaving that shows what one is feeling or thinking *(adjective)*

Audiotape   a narrow tape used to record sound that can be played back *(noun)*

Auditorium   a room where a group can gather for a school assembly or other event *(noun)*

Automatic transmission   a gearbox in a car or truck that shifts gears as the vehicle goes faster without the driver operating the gears *(noun)*

Average   not out of the ordinary *(adjective)*

Ballot   a piece of paper on which a person marks her or his choice in voting *(noun)*

Benefits   advantages; things that are good or helpful *(noun)*

Bigamy   when someone is married to more than one person at the same time *(noun)*

Bill of sale   a document showing the terms of purchase *(noun)*

Brands   products made by particular manufacturers or known by particular names *(noun)*

Bribe   money given to a person in order to influence his or her actions *(noun)*

Certificate   a paper, card, or other document showing that some-one has done something *(noun)*

City council   the group of people who govern a city *(noun)*

City   a large town; a place where many people and businesses are located *(noun)*

Civil rights laws   laws that prevent others from taking away something that is owed a person or a group of people *(noun)*

Civil service   having to do with working for the government *(adjective)*

Classified   put into groups according to some system *(adjective)*

Clients   people who use a lawyer *(noun)*

Co-sign   to sign a legal document promising to repay the money owed if the first signer does not pay; often a parent co-signs for an adult child *(verb)*

Code   a written collection of laws *(noun)*

Commercial   having to do with business *(adjective)*

Complaint   an expression of dissatisfaction or pain *(noun)*

Concealed   hidden or kept out of sight *(adjective)*

Conflict   to act against *(verb)*

Cons   arguments in opposition *(noun)*

Consequences   results of an action *(noun)*

Consumer   anyone who buys or uses goods or services *(noun)*

Contract   an agreement *(noun)*

Control   to have power over *(verb)*

Cookware   pots and pans *(noun)*

Credit   buying products or services with delayed payment or money that is loaned *(noun)*

Crime   an act that one does or doesn't do that breaks the law *(noun)*

Custody   the care, supervision, and control of someone *(noun)*

Customs   things that have been done for a long time and are widely accepted *(noun)*

Date rape   the crime of forcing a person one knows to submit to sex *(noun)*

Defects   flaws in something; imperfections *(noun)*

Defendant   the accused person or party *(noun)*

Delinquent   offending by neglect of duty or violation of duty or of law *(adjective)*

Demonstration   a meeting or parade of many people to show how they feel about something *(noun);* or showing how to do something *(noun)*

Diploma   an official paper given to a student by a school; it shows that the student has completed the required courses *(noun)*

Disability   a condition of not being able to do something *(noun)*

Disabled   unable to move, act, or work in a normal way *(adjective)*

Discipline   having to do with orderly conduct or behavior *(adjective)*

Discrimination   unfair outlook, action, or treatment based on class or category *(noun)*

Dishonorably discharged   released from the armed services in disgrace *(adjective)*

Disruptive   upsetting, bothersome, or disturbing *(adjective)*

Disturbance   a lot of noise that interrupts the peace *(noun)*

Drunk driver   someone whose driving is affected by alcohol or drugs *(noun)*

Due process   fair treatment for anyone in the court system *(noun)*

Election   the act of making a choice *(noun)*

Emancipated   released from parental care and responsibility *(adjective)*

Employer   a person or company that provides a job that pays money *(noun)*

Employment agencies   places whose business is to find jobs for people seeking them *(noun)*

Employment contract   an agreement on the conditions of employment *(noun)*

Enforceable   able to make people obey *(adjective)*

Estimate   guess; figure the approximate value of something *(verb)*

Eviction   putting a tenant out by legal process *(noun)*

Evidence   facts or things used to prove something in court *(noun)*

Exceptions   cases to which rules do not apply *(noun)*

Expert   a person who has great knowledge or skill in a certain area *(noun)*

Felonies   crimes for which the punishment may be one year or more in prison; a felony is more serious than a misdemeanor *(noun)*

Finance charge   additional money owed to a lender for borrowing money *(noun)*

Forbids   prevents; bans *(verb)*

Freight   the cost paid to transport goods *(noun)*

Full warranty   a promise to repair the sold item or replace it free of charge if something goes wrong within an indicated amount of time *(noun)*

Goods   products *(noun)*

Gossip   chatty talk *(noun)*

Grafts   pieces of skin, bone, or other living tissue that are taken from one body and set into another so as to grow and become permanent parts of the new location *(noun)*

Guarantee   a promise to replace something sold if it does not work or last as it should *(noun)*

Guardian   one who has the care of a person or property of another *(noun)*

Guideline   something that instructs, controls, or directs *(noun)*

Guilt   the feeling of having done something wrong *(noun)*

Hearing   a session in which witnesses are heard and testimony is taken; an opportunity to be heard *(noun)*

Home school   a school set up at home by parents who usually serve as teachers *(noun)*

Housing codes   body of laws set down in a clear and orderly way to regulate housing *(noun)*

Illegally   not done legally; against the law *(adverb)*

Imagine   to make up a picture or idea in the mind *(verb)*

Income tax return   a form on which you write how much money you made and how much you owe in taxes to the government for the year *(noun)*

Income   the amount of money or pay earned or received *(noun)*

Incompatible   not capable of getting along well together *(adjective)*

Informal   not following fixed rules *(adjective)*

Innocent   blameless; free from guilt *(adjective)*

Inspect   to look at carefully *(verb)*

Instructor   teacher *(noun)*

Insufficient   not enough *(adjective)*

Interest   money paid for the use of someone's money *(noun)*

Intoxicated   drunk *(adjective)*

Investigate   to look at or study carefully; to examine *(verb)*

Irresponsible   behaving in a way that can harm others; not dependable *(adjective)*

Juror   a member of a jury *(noun)*

Jury   a group of people who are chosen to listen to facts and evidence in a trial and decide the outcome of the case *(noun)*

Laid off   put out of work, especially for a short time *(verb)*

Landlord   the person who owns a house or apartment and rents it to tenants *(noun)*

Lawyer referral service   the name of a place to call to find a lawyer *(noun)*

Lease   a contract between a landlord and tenant for use of property such as an apartment or house *(noun)*

Legal   dealing with the law *(adjective)*

Legislature   a group of people with the power to make and change laws *(noun)*

License   a paper, card, or other document showing that someone is permitted by law to do something *(noun)*

Lie detector   a machine that tests if you are telling the truth when you answer questions; also called a polygraph *(noun)*

Limited warranty   a promise to repair or replace certain parts of a sold item if something goes wrong, including restrictions on what part or parts and the time frame *(noun)*

Make   a brand or type of car *(noun)*

Manual transmission   a gearbox in a car or truck that requires the driver to shift gears by pushing the clutch down by foot while shifting gears by hand *(noun)*

Manufacturer   someone who makes goods in large amounts *(noun)*

Marriage counselor   one who gives advice about marriage *(noun)*

Mental retardation an abnormal slowness of thought, development, or progress *(noun)*

Mental   having to do with the mind *(adjective)*

Minimum   the smallest amount or number that is possible *(adjective)*

Minor   a person who is under the age for being an adult according to the law *(noun)*

Miranda rights   the rights that must be explained before an arrested person can be questioned *(noun)*

Misdemeanors   crimes for which the punishment may be less than one year in prison; a misdemeanor is less serious than a felony *(noun)*

Misleading   leading in a wrong direction or in a mistaken direction or belief, often by deliberate deceit *(adjective)*

Model number   a number which tells the type or design of a product *(noun)*

Model   a style or design *(noun)*

Narrator   a person who tells what is happening in a story *(noun)*

Neglect   lack of care; too little attention *(noun)*

Odometer   instrument in a motor vehicle recording the mileage it has been driven *(adjective)*

Ordinances   local laws or regulations *(noun)*

Payroll   having to do with a list of employees who are to be paid *(adjective)*

Peers   people of the same worth; equals *(noun)*

Penalty   a punishment required by law *(noun)*

Personality   having to do with all the qualities of behavior that make a person different from other people *(adjective)*

Physical   having to do with the body rather than the mind *(adjective)*

Plaintiff   the accusing person or party *(noun)*

Politician   a person who is elected to a government office *(noun)*

Polls   places where people go to vote in an election *(noun)*

Possessions things that a person owns; personal property *(noun)*

Pregnant having an unborn child growing within the body *(adjective)*

Privacy the condition of being hidden from the view of others; secrecy *(noun)*

Private applying to individual matters, not public ones *(adjective)*

Private school a school that is set up, controlled, and mostly paid for without government money *(noun)*

Privileges special rights, favors, or advantages that are given to some person or group *(noun)*

Probation a time period when a person convicted of a crime is allowed to stay out of jail; someone supervises the person *(noun)*

Procedure the rules and methods of carrying out a legal action *(noun)*

Products things that are made by someone to sell to other people *(noun)*

Promotion an advance in rank, level, or position *(noun)*

Property something that is owned *(noun)*

Pros arguments in favor *(noun)*

Public the people as a whole *(noun)*

Public school a free school paid for by taxes and controlled by a government *(noun)*

Public services services provided for all people *(noun)*

Qualifications any skills, experience, or special training that make a person fit for a particular job *(verb)*

Qualified having the skills or experience that are needed *(adjective)*

Qualify to be fit for some particular work *(verb)*

Questionnaire a list of questions used in gathering information from people *(noun)*

Receipt a written notice that payment was received for a product or service *(noun)*

Records written evidence *(noun)*

Register to enter your name into an official record as being qualified to vote; a requirement for voting *(verb)*

Rehabilitate to restore to a former state *(verb)*

Reject refuse to take *(verb)*

Relationship attachment between two people *(noun)*

Represent to act or speak for *(verb)*; or to describe or identify *(verb)*

Reputation   good name; overall quality as seen by other people *(noun)*

Reveals   uncovers; opens up to view *(verb)*

Rodents   animals that have sharp front teeth for gnawing, such as mice or rats *(noun)*

Rural   having to do with the country or the people who live there *(adjective)*

Sanitary   free from germs and dirt *(adjective)*

School officials   people who work for a school; for example, the teachers, principal, and security guards *(noun)*

Security   related to freedom from danger, fear, or doubt *(adjective)*

Security deposit   payment given to secure rented property; usually the amount is one month's rent; the money is used in case the tenant damages the apartment or moves *(noun)*

Separate   to live apart or go in different directions *(verb)*

Serial number   an identification number *(noun)*

Sign language interpreters   people who use hand movements, instead of spoken words, to talk *(noun)*

Simple assault   use of force or a physical attack that is not serious *(noun)*

Single-parent family   a family with one parent who takes care of the family without the other parent *(adjective)*

Skills   things you do that come from training and practice *(noun)*

Skit   a short play *(noun)*

Skydiving   the sport of jumping from an airplane and falling freely for some time before opening a parachute *(noun)*

Social Security   money the federal government pays to people when they retire *(noun)*

Social Security Disability   a government program that provides money to people who are disabled and unable to work *(noun)*

Suburbs   places that are near the outskirts of a city *(noun)*

Summons   an order to appear somewhere or to do something *(noun)*

Support   to pay the cost of; to provide for *(verb)*

Suspects   people someone thinks of as probably guilty of some wrong action *(noun)*

Tenant the person renting and living in a house or apartment *(noun)*

Tester person giving a test *(noun)*

Testify to talk about a case, under oath, in a court of law *(verb)*

Testimony a solemn declaration, made usually verbally, by a witness under oath in response to questioning by a lawyer or authorized public official *(noun)*

Trade-in something such as a car which is turned in as payment or part-payment for a purchase *(noun)*

Traffic violations actions which break laws concerning the vehicles or people moving along a route *(noun)*

Truancy failure of a student to attend school *(noun)*

Tutor a teacher who teaches one student at a time *(noun)*

Typical standard; regular *(adjective)*

Under the influence affected by something such as drugs or alcohol *(adjective)*

Unemployment insurance an agreement that government made that provides money to employees who are not at fault for losing their jobs *(noun)*

Unfaithfulness breaking a promise or vow; being untrue to a person *(noun)*

Uniformed wearing an official police uniform *(adjective)*

Union a group of workers who came together to promote and protect their interests *(noun)*

Unpolluted not spoiled by trash; clean *(adjective)*

Urine a liquid waste product of the body *(noun)*

Utility a useful service or product such as water, gas, electricity, or telephone service provided to the public *(noun)*

Vacancy a place such as an apartment that is not occupied *(noun)*

Veteran's benefits money the federal government pays to those who have served in the armed forces *(noun)*

Victims people who are hurt, suffer a loss, or are killed *(noun)*

Violate to break or fail to keep a rule, law, or promise *(verb)*

Violent showing or acting with great force that causes damage or injury *(adjective)*

Visual   having to do with seeing *(adjective)*

Volunteer   to render a service without being required to do so *(verb)*

Warranty   a promise that a product will work properly or the maker or seller will repair or replace it *(noun)*

Welfare   money the federal government pays to people in need *(noun)*

Workers' Compensation   a government program that provides money to employees who are unable to work because of being hurt while on the job, regardless of fault *(noun)*

Index